MORE PRAISE FOR BURL HALL'S INSPIRING CALL TO HEAL OUR WOUNDED NATURE, *SOPHIA'S WEB*

Sophia's Web is a most wonderful and inspiring book, incandescent with personal visionary experience and words that communicate in prose that is often poetry. It is offered to us by Burl and Merry Hall both as a revelation of Sophia as Divine Source and Container of all and, drawing on the work of outstanding scientists, the clear elucidation of a new paradigm of reality that supports this revelation. Knowing that we are all embraced by Sophia's Web of Life could lift us out of our enslavement to the old dualistic patterns, old divisive beliefs and habits that are derived from fear and that now need to be transformed in a splendid affirmation of love for all creation. As they write: we need to awaken to the realization that "We are *all* a unity in the Godhead."

~Anne Baring, author of The Dream of the Cosmos: A Quest for the Soul

I've long enjoyed the energy and heart that Burl Hall brings to his article postings at Opednews.com. *Sophia's Web* weaves together Burl's unique, heartful vision, in the process, taking it to a new level. Though non-fiction, the book has been written so it draws the reader in and induces a story trance in a spiritual and artistic way. Hall weaves his words beautifully, while bringing in ideas from such luminaries as Jung and Rumi. Indeed, Hall seems to have taken Rumi so deeply into his heart and spirit that there were points in *Sophia's Web* where I thought "That's Rumi speaking!" This book pulls together the holistic Earth-Wisdom of many physicists, philosophers, psychologists, and myths. This book will inspire you, get you thinking in new, out of the box ways and give you hope for the future of humanity within us all.

~Rob Kall, Editor of OpEd Magazine

In *Sophia's Web,* Burl Hall has masterfully articulated a long overdue vision of human evolutionary transformation found reflected within the inherent integrity of Creation itself. This is a book of deep scholarship and heart. It is a purposefully passionate proposal for humanity to once again 'humanize' itself by reclaiming Gaian consciousness as our birthright—a birthright inspired by the perennial wisdom of a planetary Goddess culture. It is a work of great merit–I highly recommend it!

~ Don Oscar Miro-Quesada, co-author, Lessons in Courage: Peruvian Shamanic Wisdom for Everyday Life and founder of The Heart of the Healer (THOTH) Foundation

Sophia's Web is a passionate call to heal the destructive divides of modern life and embrace a unified cosmos rendered once again whole, told from the fiery depths of personal experience, mythology, philosophy, and science.

~ Kenneth Worthy, author of Invisible Nature: Healing the Destructive Divide between People and the Environment

Sophia's web is "His" tory and "Her" story woven together with contemporary and ancient texts, personal visions, dreams, and philosophical study. It embodies a whole new approach to "Charlotte's Web," bringing up to date the core of the separation, whether it be animal, human, insect, Earth, or the Cosmos. The oneness of the divine in all, and the equal value of every being is portrayed, whether the "femininity" of Mary Magdalene/Jesus, or the "masculinity" of Shiva/Kali. Reverent and irreverent, raw and refined, with a rigorous intellectual, emotional, and spiritual work-out, it is revealing and authentic!

~ *Cynthia Piano, Creator of Oneness House*

Sophia's Web

A Passionate Call To Heal Our Wounded Nature

Burl Benson Hall
With Merry Stetson Hall

Foreword by Carolyn Baker

Dedicated to Sophia, The Spirit of Wisdom,
My lifelong friend and mentor

Acknowledgements

I n deep gratitude, we wish to honor the many people who have contributed their wisdom and artistry to *Sophia's Web*.

Carolyn Baker, Author of *Collapsing Consciously: Transformative Truths For Turbulent Times* provided the foreword. www.carolynbaker.net

Pamela Matthews contributed the beautifully evocative cover art from her original painting *"Sophia - Peace Through Wisdom"* Copyright ©Pamela Matthews 1982 Used by permission pamela@grail.co.nz www.grail.co.nz

Meryl Ann Butler designed the stunning cover. www.merylannbutler.com

Maureen Peat of Pari Publishing donated professional editing.
maureen@paripublishing.com

Patricia Morrison provided ongoing and intensive moral support and marketing advice. www.innerfireouterlight.com

Ned Lightner of Insight Maine has created a beautiful video trailer for the book. www.insightme.com

Art Johnson of New World Communications gave us immeasurable support and guidance on creating the **www.envisionthismedia.com** website where we feature *Sophia's Web*. www.newworldcom.com artatnwc@gmail.com

Jill Piper of Lasting Image Photography in Minot, Maine created the author photograph. www.lastingimagephoto. net

Barbara Russell is our Marketing Agent

Jessica Rogers is our Proofreader

The numerous scholars, authors, mystics, and poets listed in the bibliography have deeply informed my understanding and vision for this book.

You, dear Reader, complete the circle of communication by adding your unique perception of Sophia's Wisdom to the store of Earth Wisdom.

Sophia, the Spirit of Wisdom, has inspired and guided me in writing this book and, indeed, in my whole life.

Foreword

$\mathcal{A}$s all of life on earth confronts the possibility of near-term extinction resulting from catastrophic climate change, and as only a small number of the human species takes personal responsibility for creating a planet that is becoming increasingly uninhabitable, many are frantically searching for new ideas that will reverse or minimize the consequences of our predicament. Surely, humans are capable of discovering a new technological fix or constructing a new paradigm that will spare us from terminating life on earth, aren't they? Yet as my friend and mentor Michael Meade notes, it is not so much new ideas that are needed in times of decline, but rather, a radical return to ancient wisdom. In fact, our current predicament is a direct result of forsaking timeless truths that when lived with integrity and passion preclude the possibility of perceiving ourselves as separate from all other living beings. When our unequivocal oneness with them is recognized, it becomes impossible to objectify them or relate to them in a hierarchical or possessive fashion.

Inherent in the ancient wisdom of which I speak is the principle of inter-connectedness, or inter-being, if you will—a notion with which timeless myths and stories are replete. What is more, no mythological character depicts this inter-connectedness more vividly than Sophia.

According to Jungian analyst, Marion Woodman, "*Sophia is the archetypal image of the feminine principle and thus partner to the masculine god. She is present in all traditions, mythologies, and religions – in Hinduism she is Shakti, in Egyptian myth she is called Isis. Traditionally it is in the gnostic, mystical, and alchemical traditions that the feminine face of the divine is central and present.*"

Characteristic of Sophia and the feminine principle is not the linear modus operandi of the goal-directed masculine, but rather, a web-like, inclusive embrace of all that is. Somewhere in the twentieth century, a little boy named Burl Hall began at a very early age to grasp this web, and now in 2014 he is joyously entangled in it. So entangled is he that he was compelled to write *Sophia's Web: A Passionate Call to Heal Our Wounded Nature.*

Sophia's Web is the saga of Hall's journey from fleeting visions of Sophia in childhood to a mature, surrendered embrace of the Sacred Feminine which now underpins and informs his life, his work, and his connection with the earth community. "My primary belief," writes Hall, "is that the Goddess is the power by which all are born, maintained, and dissolved. It is she who weaves the entire web of life."

Rarely do we have the opportunity to hear an embodied male acknowledge what the author lays bare in this book. Almost effortlessly he was able to acknowledge, at an early age, not only the feminine principle in the world but the feminine within himself. As with any male socialized within the context of industrial civilization, Hall experienced societal pressure to embrace the patriarchal perspective which prizes a way of life based on power and control. Yet *Sophia's Web* reveals a man who has moved through and beyond patriarchal programming to an integration of the feminine principle within himself and who strives to apply Sophia's wisdom in his life and work. Clearly, she is never far from his consciousness as we hear so incisively in these words:

> *Everywhere I look, I see her. I see her in the images arising, dancing and returning to the font of my mind and in the imagined form of my body. I further realize her as my body's ability to heal and to die. I know her as the life-supporting manure nourishing flowers in their growth, as well as in the flowers that grow and the agent behind their growth and dissolution. I know her in the Worm that nourishes them from below as well as the Sun that nourishes them from above. I further realize her as defining the relationship of flowers to the ecosystems at large. I then experience her in the microscopic atomic world, as well as in the incomprehensible number of stars in the nighttime sky. Everything existing within or without has its ground in my beloved Mother. She smiles at our notions of personal and impersonal God and disintegrates them into dust. When the dust clears, only Sophia remains. She alone is real for her essence is reflected in all her creations.*

On a planet unfathomably raped, pillaged, and plundered by humans as a result of contempt for the feminine principle and enchantment with all things patriarchal, Burl and his wife, Merry, beautifully articulate why at this point in our demise, only a collective and individual return to Sophia's web and wisdom can prevent us from eliminating all life on earth. Patriarchy's linear, binary thinking causes us to abhor web-like patterns, moist with the natural secretions of the all-inclusive feminine. Rather, modernity prizes "clear thinking," "a direct course of action," and the avoidance of anything resembling Sophia's "sticky web." Thus the human ego protests chaos, uncertainty, and interdependence. Yet Sophia within every human being, that is to say, the divine self at our core, as well as Sophia in the world, now stands before us demanding that we willingly enter her web, and the cacophony of her screams compels us to surrender to a different and decidedly radical kind of power—not power *over*, but power *with* all of life and the earth community.

Burl Hall reminds us of Sigmund Freud's profound and prophetic conclusion that *"mankind will not put aside its sickness and its discontent until it is able to abolish every dualism."* Hence the core purpose of this book which the author states so clearly: "This book's purpose, then, is to bring peace through the integration of seemingly opposing forces." In order to achieve this peace, much emotional and spiritual work is required, but in *Sophia's Web*, Burl and Merry Hall tantalize us with the rewards of doing that work and compel us to embrace the journey with Sophia, for indeed our lives and our planet depend on it.

Carolyn Baker, Boulder Colorado
Author of *Collapsing Consciously: Transformative Truths For Turbulent Times*
www.carolynbaker.net

Contents

Acknowledgements   ix

Foreword   xi

Introduction   xix

PART I   *Marriage of the Personal to the Divine*   1

Chapter 1   Dualism and Holism   3
     Dualistic and Objectified Thinking   4
     Holographic and Metaphorical
     Thinking   7

Chapter 2   The Woman with No Name   11
     Virgin Birth   16
     Imagery Exercise: Natural Wisdom   18
     Adult Dream of Flying
     Above the Earth   23

Chapter 3   Naming the Nameless   27
     Forest Dream   28
     Synchronicity   33
     Naming as Co-Creating   36

Chapter 4   Revealing the Cosmic Child   39
                  Dream: Ghost of Lost Friend   42
                  Spirals   45
                  Vision: Inside the Web   47
                  Both-And   48

PART II   *Lifting Sophia's Veil*   51

Chapter 5   The Web of Life   53
                  Scientists and Mystics on
                  the Web of Life   55
                  Quantum Physics   57
                  Poets and Artists on Holism   57
                  Re-Membering Who We Are   59

Chapter 6   Mirror, Mirror In Us All   61
                  Replacing a Mindset of Violence   62
                  Linguistics and Logic   64
                  Traditional and
                  Metaphorical Logic   65
                  Metaphorical Significance
                  of Sexuality   68
                  Bohm, Pribram, and the
                  Holomovement   69
                  Fourier Transforms   75

Chapter 7   Cosmic Sex   79
                  Marrying Athena   80
                  Human and Divine Conception   82
                  Children of Mother Nature   87
                  Global Creation Stories   89

Chapter 8   The Ocean of Life   95
             The Ocean Metaphor
               in Various Cultures   99
             Ancient and Modern
               Cave Rituals   103
             Fear of Nature, Women,
               and Chaos   106

PART III   *Evolving Towards Wholeness*   113

Chapter 9   Transcendence Revisited   115
             Parable: Bensophia   116
             Giving Birth   121
             Transforming Our View
               of Darkness   123
             The Star of David   126

Chapter 10   Ecstasy and Nature   129
             The Dance of the Seven Veils:
               In Search of Ecstasy   132
             Finding Our True Nature   135
             Source of Evil   138

Chapter 11   The Tangled Web We Weave   141
             Denunciation of the Goddess   144
             Of Witches and Cats   146
             Cinderella   148
             Adam and Eve   150

Chapter 12   The Lovely Web She Weaves   155
     Paradigm Shift to a
     Partnership Model   157
     Beyond War   159
     Designed for Love   164
     Of King Oedipus, King Herod,
     and King Culture   167
     The Return of the Divine Child   168

Chapter 13   Awakening to Wholeness   173
     Vision: One Soul   174
     Unity of Science, Myth,
     and Religion   178
     You Are Anointed by God   185

Bibliography   187

Burl's Request of the Reader   193

Introduction

O' let me teach you how to knit again
this scattered corn into one mutual sheaf,
these broken limbs again into one body.
–Shakespeare, Titus Andronicus, V, iii

We are each woven with threads of Love into the web of all being. This book follows the threads of that web as they spread throughout all aspects of our lives and our universe. It explores them on multiple levels:

- Personal, using my experience as an example
- Intellectual, drawing on the works of philosophers
- Cultural, exploring mythology and literature
- Scientific, exploring systems and holographic theories
- Spiritual, examining the vision of the great mystics of the world's religions

The name, Sophia, means *God's Wisdom* in the Greek translations of ancient Hebrew writings. Sophia, the Goddess of Wisdom, is given many names in many different cultures, including but not limited to Athena, Tara, Inanna, Hochmah, Isis, Ma'at, Aluna, Thinking Woman, Kali, Shakti, Astarte and Tiamat. She is the Woman with a Thousand Faces.

Solomon wrote of this divine Wisdom Goddess:
*She reaches mightily from one end of the Earth to the other
And while remaining in herself, she renews all things....
And orders all things well...*
    –Book of the Wisdom of Solomon 7:27; 8:1

By whatever name we call Wisdom, she appears universally, underlying all creation. She dwells in you, in me, in all humankind, indeed, in all beings. *Sophia's Web* is a celebration of Wisdom as she is witnessed in nature, science, all spiritual traditions, and throughout the universe. It celebrates that infinity of Wisdom manifest within us all.

My purpose in publishing *Sophia's Web* is to explore the incredibly intricate and beautiful web into which Wisdom has woven everything, including us. Becoming aware of this unity within diversity is crucial in today's world, in which dualism—with its attendant greed, violence, and alienation—presents a threat to our sanity, peace, and biosphere.

This book is part of a holographic movement that is now gaining momentum. That movement integrates several factors: a new science based on wholeness (Capra, 1975), the growing recognition of the feminine godhead (Baring and Cashford, 1991), a growing awareness of the wisdom of the mystics of all traditions (Campbell, 1990), and the conscious evolution movement. It draws upon the wisdom of such revolutionary, historic intellects as Goethe, Steiner, and Jung. What I see in these diverse perspectives is a unity. The contents of this book draw on Wisdom as she reveals herself in the works of these scholars, as she manifests in my own life, and–by extension–as she lives in the hearts of my readers.

I offer *Sophia's Web* to help bring peace through the integration of seemingly opposing forces. No force is defeated, just as no energy ever dies but is simply transformed and re-integrated into the living energy of the universe. Once we realize our true, holographic relationship to the universe, we are empowered to heal the alienation of the individual and prevent the destruction of the Earth. Ultimately, I hope *Sophia's Web* will help the reader realize that all the various religions and sciences are currently speaking the same thought in an infinitely varied number of ways. All we have to do to see this unity-in-diversity is to open our eyes a little. The world we live in, for all her imperfections and contradictions, is our uni-versity.

As a stripper teasingly removes her clothing to reveal her naked beauty, God's Wisdom will reveal her essence to you by stripping away the layers of the surface world, which would include yourself as a separate ego. This revelation will be that of the naked Truth shining brightly in the depths of your being. In that Truth, you will know yourself, the world and that which is beyond the world. Interestingly, it will not be some foreign creature you will find standing naked. It will be *your* Truth standing naked, unveiled at the core of your being. Fear not, for in that nakedness you will discover your true power and beauty. This is the nudity of great art, not of shameful pornography. Let the journey begin!

Part 1 ~
Marriage of the Personal to the Divine

Chapter 1
Dualism and Holism

And the twain shall be one flesh:
so then they are no more twain, but one flesh.
~ Mark 10:8

*A*nd on the 8th day (today!) God said, "Let there be evolution!" Why do those words come forth? Because, we are on the brink of disaster, perhaps even extinction, due to a dualistic philosophy, a way of looking at life, that doesn't work. We think only of ourselves–our wealth, our security, and our convenience– in this day and age. While we fret over our own personal future, we forget how our children and posterity will live. We destroy the wellbeing of our Mother Earth.

We are experiencing various religious and political groups warring with one another to the point of bloodshed, heartbreak, hatred, and death. Each political or religious group calls the other an "evil doer" while being blinded to seeing themselves in the eyes of those evildoers. While these groups are diverse, they suffer one illness, self-centeredness. Both sides of each conflict (coin) are blind to the unity of humanity.

In search of ever more resources and production, we rape and pillage our Mother Earth. We are destroying our environment because we have gotten ourselves into a competitive framework. We see winning as having more access to resources and goods than someone else. This competitive mindset results in a depletion of natural resources. Our ultimate goal is to win dominance over Nature, yet that war is exposed to be against ourselves. Our relationship to Nature, after all, is the same as that of a child to its mother. We are dependent on her for survival. What shall we breathe when we destroy the atmosphere? Is it wise for us to take a dagger to the womb that supports us?

If you don't agree with the reality of Global Warming, listen to the reports of increased dead zones in the oceans. Why, there is even the reemergence of poisonous algae that went extinct millions of years ago in these areas! This "devolution" proves that nothing is truly gone. Perhaps what we think is extinct is but in sleep, a potential waiting to unfold. It is only our human arrogance that thinks we are top of the line. All that appears linear to us, including evolution, may well be cyclical, just as the Earth proved to be round, not flat.

There is, furthermore, a widening gap worldwide between the rich and the poor who are becoming more and more like slaves. Yet, if we attend to history, we discover that slaves tend to rebel. Their fear of being beaten, starved and killed serves as the catalyst for anger and revolution. The fear of this happening also enslaves the slaveholder, who is consumed by the effort to thwart such "terrorism." Oppression breeds rebellion; rebellion breeds more oppression. Round and round we go in a vicious cycle. When will it stop?

DUALISTIC AND OBJECTIFIED THINKING

These issues reflect an underlying philosophy called *dualism* that pits one thing against the other. Two men holding guns out at each other are said to be in a duel. Either you live and I die, or I live and you die. Such duels are a metaphor for our dualistic philosophy of life. Insanely we pit our views against one another. Hence, in today's world, we have multiple wars, neurotic and psychotic illnesses, the battle of the sexes and rape.

All of this turmoil results from a dualistic philosophy. We are so egocentric that we cannot see the various ways of perceiving the world as being akin to multiple spokes on the same wheel. Spokes appear to be going in diametrically opposite directions. Yet all spokes are necessary to the whole wheel turning in its own holistic cycles towards a goal neither the left nor the right spoke can fathom. Many of the world's wars (or glorified duels) would disappear if we could accept an overriding truth: what is diverse is unified.

For example, animals have different ways of perceiving from humans and hence live in a different world. There are some birds that have the visual capacity to see upwards of 500 miles. Meanwhile we often struggle to see 90 miles ahead as we sit atop a mountain on a clear, sunny day. However, in our self-centered world, neither bird nor human give much credence to the other's point of view.

Even within our own species, we are egocentric in our views of the world. We fail to see that spokes, which begin on opposite sides of a circle nonetheless, lead to one hub. We each tend to see our specific way of viewing the world as *the* way; we really don't get that our way is simply *a* way. We are now reaching the "dead end" of our "one way" streets.

Yet, each way of perceiving from every individual in every species reflects God, just as the multitudes of colors we see are all refractions of one source of light, our sun. Imagine how "reality" would seem different if we could see ultraviolet and infrared, for instance. What if we could hear the rumblings of the inner Earth and the music of the dancing stars?

Alternatively, consider that perhaps we can! Perhaps we just don't know how to look and how to listen past what we believe to be real. Perhaps we have much to learn from animals like bats that taught us radar. Such enhanced perceptions may be in our evolutionary future as well as in our indigenous past.

Human perceptions change according to the physiology, psychology and spirituality of an individual within a cultural framework. We "see" what we are taught to expect and to value. There is no objective reality "out there" that is being observed by detached and rational minds. For example, rather than history being an objective science filled with facts, the study of the past is a function of the perceptions of the historian. These perceptions are determined by personal, familial, social, cultural and biological variants. For instance, the focus on war, politics, economics, and material invention taught in American schools as "history" overlooks art, labor, women, home and philosophy. This is because of what our mainstream culture values. Ultimately, it is these values that determine how we see everything in the world, from gender and sexuality to world politics to the universe at large. These values are the children born of a union between our perceptions, brought to us by our lim-ited senses–such as sight, smell and taste–and our distorted philosophies, shaped by their words, beliefs, and culture that surround us.

Over the course of history, our views of the world have changed because our philosophies and perceptions have changed. In past cultures and societies, people were very comfortable with the language of myths, fairy tales and dreams. By contrast, in today's world, we are more apt to believe in what we deem to be the literal language of sci-entists and scholars. Similarly, the ancient cultures could see energy or spirit patterns in the land that mirrored the energy patterns in the body. Shamans could use the synergy between these energies for healing both the individual and the Earth. Today, we sometimes see this ability as nonsensical and superstitious. These shifts do not occur because our minds have progressed in how they see the world. Rather, the shifts simply reflect cultural changes in philosophy and perception that have implications for how we interact with the world.

Within the context of modern literal thought, our language focuses on a specific definition of a subject that ultimately isolates that subject from its related verb, from the whole, and from the thinker. To the degree that we can isolate and *objectify* what we perceive, we can fool ourselves that we are merely *objective* observers, non-interactive with what we observe. We become "nominal" thinkers, cut off from the changes actively unfolding around us.

This trend towards literalism or objectification is a mirror of the scientific philosophy of reductionism, which interprets the universe as divisible into its basic parts in order to understand how things work. From a reductionist and literal point of view, a tree would be nothing more than a tree, existing in isolation from the rest of the universe. Its metaphorical relationship to the greater whole and the ecological interdependence of the tree with the other aspects of its eco-region would be ignored.

HOLOGRAPHIC AND METAPHORICAL THINKING

Within the metaphorical world of dreams, myths and legends, this same tree would have symbolic significance that spoke to the spiritual, physical and psychological essence of an individual and to the universe at large. We find, for instance, the tree-of-life symbol existing in varied cultural myths. It appears in the well known ancient Jewish story in Genesis, Native American mythology and teachings, stories of the !Kung bushmen of Africa, and as a symbol from ancient Irish shamanist cultures existing prior to the Druids. In the senses of the people living in ancient cultures, a tree's existence had meaning in relationship to the individual observing it and to the greater whole, both visible and invisible.

Such significance cannot be dismissed as "mere" metaphor. Epistemologist Gregory Bateson (2000) defines metaphor as a language that connects the apparently disparate. He further asserts that metaphor is Nature's language, our own mother tongue. Fantasies and dreams are written in the language of metaphor. Because of the rich, connective tissue of such language, fantasies and dreams, like myths and fairy tales, speak more fully about the wholeness of life than what is literal. By using metaphor, one image can be universal in its reflection of things or processes. Metaphor is the holistic language of the universal matrix by which one thing is revealed in the many and many are revealed in the one.

Rudolph Steiner expresses this holographic relationship that humanity has with the universe in terms of microcosm and macrocosm:

> *The three stages of activity of the human soul - the purely intellectual, the aesthetic, and the moral -are microcosmic images of the three realms which in the macrocosm.... lie one above the other. The Astral world is reflected in the world of thought; the Devachanic world in the aesthetic sphere of pleasure and displeasure; and the Higher Devachanic world is reflected as morality (good or bad deeds). (Steiner, 1911, p.16)*

Mythologist Joseph Campbell's work, *The Hero of a Thousand Faces* (1990), realizes this holographic matrix in the metaphorical language of myth. As the title suggests, Campbell's thesis is that there is one hero with different faces in different cultures. Each culture tells a different myth enfolding

8

and unfolding the same Truth. When we read deeply into Campbell's work, we eventually realize that each of us is an individual face of the one hero. Our heroic task is to discover that hero leading his life deep within us. Hence the ultimate cry of the hero reading and speaking the myth is, "I am (S)He!" Self-discovery is realizing we are a creative and unique expression of the one hero radiating a thousand faces.

This revelation of who we are in relation to the hero in myth is reflected brilliantly in Michael Ende's (1984) classic, *The Neverending Story*. It contains the story of a little boy named Bastian who comes across a book also called *The Neverending Story*. Bastian reads of a boy named Atreyu whose quest is to save a magical land called Fantasia. The land of Fantasia literally has everything you can imagine, since it is the land of creative fantasy. As Bastian reads the book, he discovers that he himself is the one to save Fantasia by ultimately naming a Child-Empress. In that quest, within the fourth dimension of imagination, to name his Empress, he finds his true identity and power in the "real," three-dimensional world, where he must face down bullies.

The demand of the great philosopher, Socrates, was to *"know thyself."* This demand saturates *The Neverending Story*. Bastian must find his true identity in the world, i.e., his Goddess, his true Nature. This quest, I would maintain, is a universal one transcending the accumulation of wealth and power.

Chapter 2
The Woman with No Name
⟶⟋⟋⟋

Change is the only constant in life.
–Heraclitus

As it was for Bastian, so it is for me. The naming of a nameless Empress mirrors a process that has manifested as I came to know and name my soul. When I first saw the movie version of *The Neverending Story*, it frustrated me that I couldn't quite "hear" the name Bastian gives his Empress. I now realize that this "flaw" was no carelessness in the film-making. It was a tool to awaken my awareness that I am Bastian and must name my own Goddess. Knowing that this story reflects my process of self-discovery has allowed me to know myself in relation to the greater whole. I now see myself in all of history. My personal drama in this day and age is timeless. In this knowledge, I have become aware of my eternal nature. This is the gift metaphor has given me. This is the power of story.

The process of being aware of the Empress-with-no-name began to unfold when I was four, perhaps five, years of age. On numerous occasions during that period of my life, I would have visions of a beautiful and awe-inspiring woman. Without warning, she would appear in the kitchen of the apartment where I lived, poised in midair or sitting on a birdcage that hung in the corner. According to adult logic, it would seem she would need to be small to fit into the corner of the kitchen. Yet, I never ascribed any size to this woman. This phenomenon continues to occur when the woman appears in my adult dreams. She appears to be all-powerful. Yet, there is never any perception of size.

The mysterious image of this woman of no size was awe-inspiring. She had golden-brown hair that flowered into ringlets and flowed in powerful waves to rest in comfort upon her gracefully curved and bare shoulders. This woman was dressed in a blue gown, of the same hue as the daytime sky. Its style appeared similar to that of women living in the 1700's. Low-cut in the front, the dress revealed the soft, rounded tops of her breasts. Cupping the breasts from underneath was a seam. From there, the gown fell in multiple folds and draped about her body. Appearing from the bottom hem of the gown were the woman's unclad feet. From the bareness of the feet, to the style of the hair and dress, the entire image of this woman produced an atmosphere of naturalness. This perception also elicited an impression that she was an ancient being.

At rare times, this woman appeared with two other ladies. These women were identical to her in style of appearance and demeanor. These three did not seem to be in any type of power relationship. There were no bosses in this trio. Rather, they all seemed synchronized in their objective, which had something to do with me. This objective is still an unraveling mystery to me. The power of these women was intense and singular. The trio, together, exuded one radiant power, a fiery field of light and love in which I felt enveloped.

When the central woman appeared alone, I realized she had created me and monitored my progression in life. She knew everything about me, even my most private thoughts. This sense of being monitored created an awareness of an intense presence. Her eyes appeared to penetrate to the core of my being. I was forever naked before her stare.

I did not call the woman a Goddess. I only learned this term much later, living as I did in such a patriarchal culture. With a child's innocence, I only considered her my friend. Indeed, I never found it curious that she didn't have a name. Yet, as an adult, something impelled me to name her.

When she appeared, I would be very still. My friend's radiating power and magnificence generated a deep sense of love and commitment. Though the woman only appeared in form in the kitchen of my apartment, I could feel her presence even when not there. She was with me wherever I went—outside playing with friends, in the living room, or in the bath.

These experiences lasted about a year and eventually I learned the ways of our society. For fear of ridicule, I did not speak to anyone about my friend, not even my parents. In the world of schools, parents, and peers, there was no room to discuss the visions of a Goddess. I suppressed her memory as a silly childhood fantasy. I began to attend to what the mainstream culture was telling me was true and turned away from my heart's deepest love.

As I will illustrate throughout the book, the visions were not a silly childhood fantasy to be dismissed as "an imaginary friend." I was wrong when I allowed my society to induce me to label them such. My visions tied in with ancient mystical teachings on the Holy Mother. The power behind these visions projected an all-encompassing aware-ness transcending any cultural or social boundaries. That power was the power of everything. It even encompassed children's fantasies.

The most salient point of the visions was the intense feelings of power and awareness that the woman radiated to me. The experience of this power would continue throughout my lifetime. The utilization of a woman's form was but one way in which the woman would manifest. As I grew older, she would often use various metaphors for describing herself, sometimes cosmic, sometimes artistic, sometimes metaphysical, sometimes ritual and sometimes natural. The binding theme to these experiences was the awareness of a pure Presence or state of being, from which everything erupted, be it planet, star, poem, or dream.

As we continue with discussions on these experiences, it will become clear to the reader that each experience mirrors and contains all the previous experiences. Just as DNA mirrors the electron, my experiences mirror one another. What is more important is that my experiences mirror mystical teachings from throughout the world. Many readers may have noticed, for instance, that my visions are akin to Mother Mary's visitations to some Christian children throughout history. Occasional children in all cultures are blessed with such visions, mediated and interpreted through the beliefs of their native culture.

As my worldview matured and became less innocent, more acculturated, my experience of her became more abstracted. For example, at the age of 17, I began experiencing my life as being born here and now from an infinite state of consciousness or being. I continue to have these experiences today. I do not control them; they just happen. Describing this infinite Being is impossible, for it is beyond words, conceptualizations and thoughts.

The best way I know to relate the place in which I meet her to the reader is to describe it as a radiant and translucent darkness outshining all the suns in the universe. When sensing this state of being, I become aware of a time-less presence that envelops, dissolves, and gives birth to my entire life. I realize that my life is in a continuous process of creation and destruction within the timeless state of infin-ity. I have no past or future in this place. An instant and an eternity are one. My life appears to be analogous to a movie projected on a screen. My life's movements in time and space appear to be an illusion generated by a series of "snapshots" of projected light continually flowing from this consciousness or being.

I originally thought these experiences were an expres-sion of a temporary insanity. Since I had experimented with acid (LSD) at 17, I thought I was having "flashbacks." Today, I completely understand the meaning of these experiences when I gaze in meditation upon an image of the Hindu Goddess, *Kali,* whose name means *Black.* Her blackness tells me she is synonymous to the Roman *Matrum Noctrum,* the *Night of the Great Mother.* She is also the Greek *Nyx,* the *Uncreated Night* and *Mother of Lord Eros.* In pre-Druid Ireland, She would be the Goddess Danu, who is the foundational creative energy of the universe, existing prior to creation. Traveling about the world, these Goddesses also manifest as the Goddess *Aluna* of the Native American tribe called the Kogis. According to the Kogis, Aluna is the *darkly* Sea Goddess who thought every-thing into existence. These women are not separate. They are the translucent "darkness" of the pure state of being out of which I felt myself emerge as light. As cartoons picture characters with "bright ideas" appearing with light bulbs over their heads, I appear to be a "bright idea" of the Goddess. In accordance to the Kogis' belief in Aluna, I am a thought arising from the font of my Mother's mind. Hence, I am truly her son.

In tying all these teachings from throughout the world together, I now realize that the Bible's creation story in Genesis is about me. My experiences of the source of origin are identical to the description of the beginning in Genesis: 1:2, "And the Earth was without form and void and darkness was upon the face of the deep." When the Lord thundered from this dark and mysterious womb with his famous "*Let there be light*," I thundered right along with him. I am the lightening through which the thunder of his word becomes visible. I am the leap between conception and manifestation.

VIRGIN BIRTH

As we will discuss throughout this book, the process of arising from this darkness or no-thingness, which I often call the *unmanifest*, is the virgin birth. Christhood is not an occurrence in the past, limited only to Jesus of Nazareth. It is timeless, meaning it happens here and now. In as much as any God is virgin born, then I am virgin born. Likewise YOU are virgin born.

I also experience the virgin birth when I am at a natural setting, such as the beach or the mountains. In these relaxing natural moments, I often become cognizant of a conscious presence in the silence of Nature. The intensity and stillness of this Presence is beyond description. Neither reason nor intellect can ever comprehend this mysterious Presence. It is beyond rational thought. Presence is analogous to an intense point that is everywhere. Yet, it is non-locatable. It is an incomprehensible and vast ocean with no shores. Yet, it is smaller than a pinpoint. It is gentle and serene. Yet, it is so intense that an exploding star, in comparison, is but a mere pinprick. The entire universe appears to erupt simultaneously from Presence, as I erupted from the state of no-thingness. When realizing this birthing process, I feel myself being bathed in radiant love. I become pregnant with Love. In the tender touch of Presence, my worries and cares dissolve into oblivion. I expand beyond myself and melt into peace.

In my awareness of Presence, I further realize a subtle "HUM" about everything. Everything vibrates. The vibrations are the "HUM" that emanates from the silence of Presence. I cannot imitate this "HUM." My vocal cords cannot make the sound. I can only represent the sound by referring to it as a "HUM." I often contemplate these experiences by relating them to the following quotation from the Bible (I Kings 19:13):

...And after the Earthquake, fire.
But, Yahweh (I AM) was not in the fire.
And after the fire,
A light murmuring sound.

These lines give voice to my experience of Presence. The Biblical writer and I speak of the same being. The Orientals identify this "murmuring" sound of creation when they chant "OM." "OM" is the Word of God. In it is the All. It takes little insight to realize "OM" is the "murmur" of the Bible. When hearing the beautiful sound of that glorious word, "OM," ringing from the lips of devotees, I always envision the birth of the universe. I can feel the harmony of the cosmos, the music of the spheres. I can hear my harmony singing and dancing right along with all the planets, stars and galaxies. The world becomes wonderment. I can waft one kiss into the infinite depths of the universe and know that my kiss will fall instantaneously on the soft cheeks of a far distant star. All limitations of time and space disappear, and I experience myself as intimately connected with the entirety of the cosmos.

I have had these experiences of Presence off and on for many years now. In my opinion, the "murmur" of Kings and the "OM" of the Orient express the "hum" I heard emanating from Presence. There is but one God that does not give a hoot about our denomination. I now call this "HUM" my Father and consider him to be the creative "Word" that formed the universe.

When cognizant of Presence, I realize God as a being more magnificent and beautiful than any conception of God presented by relatives, friends and churches. In the body of Presence, I do not feel any fear of judgment. She just "hums" along, rolling through all things, forever giving birth to the world.

There have been many more experiences in my lifetime that have led to the understanding of Goddess and God presented in this book. For example, in the early 90's, I became fascinated by a work written by Dr. Bernie Siegel (1989). Dr. Siegel is a medical doctor whose work with cancer and heart patients caused him to question traditional approaches to medicine. His work challenges our traditional Western focus on the body as a repairable machine analogous to a car. Dr. Siegel argues instead that we have a natural wisdom that can heal physical, emotional and psychological maladies. According to Dr. Siegel, "tapping" into this wisdom can produce powerful and positive results in healing that put traditional medicine to shame. He argues that we can allow our body's wisdom to aid in a cure by changing our beliefs and thoughts.

IMAGERY EXERCISE: NATURAL WISDOM

Dr. Siegel's words made perfect sense to me. Ever since I can remember, I have naturally equated Nature and Wisdom. In my mind, they never were two. Nature is intelligence--not the kind of intelligence we associate with IQ scores, grades or work performance, rather, a creative intelligence that generates the human body and the entire universe out of its womb.

Influenced by the work of Dr. Siegel, I began to do "Natural Wisdom" imagery exercises in my work as a volunteer career counselor. I adhered to the theory that our "unconscious" was a pool of hidden knowledge or wisdom. This knowledge, I further believed, was perfectly natural. It was the power behind our body's ability to heal a cut finger, develop a baby, or project a dream. I believed the imageries helped activate a client's "unconscious" mind and caused her to tap into this reservoir of natural wisdom. In so doing, it could help her make a career decision.

These exercises proved extremely fruitful for those who chose to sink their hearts into them. I recall one woman completing the exercise in tears, stating she had envisioned a Woman of Light who exhibited an incomprehensible love for her. As she sat, I wondered if this woman was not tapping into something she had long forgotten. Since I had not remembered my childhood friend, discussed previously, it was I who was beginning to tap into something I had long forgotten. As we will see later, I was also beginning to develop a name for the forgotten nameless woman that appeared in my childhood. As often happens, my client/ student became my teacher, pointing the way to deeper insight and growth in me. Such is the way of Wisdom, as illustrated by Wordsworth's often quoted saying, "*The child is father of the man.*"

Wisdom manifested itself in a variety of ways to people engaged in doing these images. One woman's visions exhibited Wisdom's silly playfulness, for she appeared dressed in a safari outfit and made my client laugh. Apparently she was about to go on a wild hunt with this woman. Was this hunt for wild game? Of course not! She was the Artemis-Diana

(Lover of the Wild) of the psyche. She was the hunter for Truth and was that Truth for the client. Interestingly, this particular woman began a long process of self-exploration after these sessions. This self-exploration was the hunt.

I became fascinated by the generation of these diverse images because they reflected what each client needed to know or experience. The first woman needed to know her love. The second needed to search herself by engaging in an internal safari. Each person's needs determined how Wisdom manifested distinctively from the "unconscious."

At the time I was doing these imageries, I was not fully remembering my childhood friend. She was very "fuzzy" in my memory, a long lost, silly, childhood fantasy. As if in preparation for remembering my friend, I engaged in a self-exploration group in 1991. One important experience in this group entailed a spontaneous understanding of the generation of a thought. This experience was instrumental in developing everything you are reading in this book.

On the particular night the experience occurred, the facilitator of the group was probing to prod me into an exploration of a topic in my life. Generally, when engaged in introspection of this sort, I watch my thoughts closely because I believe they emerge from the "unconscious" and contain much rich information. This particular night, I paid attention to more than my thoughts. I attended to how they were born and from where. This was not a conscious decision on my part. It was "accidental," an incidence of the Goddess or, perhaps I might say, a synchronicity of her and my working together.

What I noticed at first was an infinite nothingness that was analogous to a brilliant darkness or emptiness. As I watched and listened to this blissful emptiness, I became disoriented and lost all sense of time and self. For a moment in eternity, I lost any sense of the group and the probing facilitator. Time stopped, and I did not know the difference between an hour and a second. While in this state, I felt a slight "power surge" in my depths, followed by a subtle "buzzing" noise. This "buzzing" energy surged and then flowered into a thought as it erupted into immediate awareness. The thought and I appeared to be born simultaneously as I again became aware of the group and the probing facilitator. I then expressed the thought in relationship to the facilitator's question.

Upon leaving the group that night, I began meditating on my experience. I related the process to a woman giving birth. Like a woman's womb from which a baby emerges, there appeared to be an invisible "womb" in the depths of my Soul which I experienced as an infinite point of singularity existing beyond time and space. It was from this point that my thoughts appeared to flow into manifestation. I further realized the thought was eternal. As an egg exists in a woman's ovaries as a potential human being from the time she was herself a fetus, the thought had existed within me as a potential insight waiting to unfold.

I also contemplated the effects of the facilitator's probe. Though she was a woman, she had served in a fathering role. Her probe functioned to fertilize the unborn thought within me and caused him to flower forth and express himself. Though I was biologically a male, I was a mother; though the facilitator was a woman, she was a father. Perhaps, I began to reason to myself, this was the reason many scholars of human behavior were saying men had a feminine side to them, an *anima*, while women had a masculine side, an *animus*.

What I was beginning to realize was that gender is not a thing. I was recognizing gender as more of a verb than a noun. (See chapter 7 for a further discussion of this insight.) The terms, *woman* and *man*, referred to function

21

and transcended the human body and personality. Human beings, I began to reason, took form as women and men because they mirrored an interactive process that was universal. The biological function of human women mirrored a process that pervades the universe: to conceive, give birth, sustain, and absorb (devour or receive) life. Similarly, the biological function of human men mirrored a process apparent throughout the universe: to penetrate, fertilize and initiate division and formation. Why else, I wondered, would the sun be seen throughout the world as a Father and the Earth as a Mother? Mom absorbs Dad's rays and conceives new life! I then realized this process mirrored my absorption of the fertilizing words of the group facilitator. It was through that absorption that I generated a thought. Why else would we call a creative idea "our baby?" *"The entire universe makes love,"* I thought to myself. Sex was no longer profane or dirty, as reflected in our modern day attitudes. It was sacred, an act of the gods.

At the time of the experience with the facilitator, I did not understand how my experience of being a "mother to thought" mirrored my experiences of Presence giving birth to the world. I was not relating the experience to the sense of the translucent darkness giving birth to my life as a "light." I also was not fully remembering my childhood friend. Yet, I eventually realized all these experiences were expressions of one insight. My experience with the facilitator was a primer for the realization of how all these various experiences tied together. I would eventually discover that just as a spider spins a web and sits in the center of it, my friend was the spider sitting in the center of this web of experiences. (Indeed, her name in the southwestern Native American stories of the Navajo, Pueblo, Tewa, Kiwa, Hopi and Cherokee tribes is Spider Grandmother.)

ADULT DREAM OF FLYING ABOVE THE EARTH

For me to begin seeing this web, my friend had to reintroduce herself to me. In the summer of 1992, I began to have a series of dreams regarding the feminine divinity. This came upon the heels of a time of deep angst and depression for me. This was also a time of deep questioning regarding how my life was going. One of the original and most powerful of the dreams occurred on a night I was feeling depressed and turbulent due to stress at work. Indeed, as the initial part of the dream reveals, I felt trapped inside an eternal pit of misery:

While drifting into sleep, feeling depressed and trapped, I found myself falling into an eternal pit. Suddenly, my arms flew above my head and I felt two hands grab hold of my wrists.

Glancing up, I saw the face of my childhood friend, dressed in her blue gown, with a face aglow with light. That smile I knew in childhood provided nourishment for me again. My friend was realized as a peace-of-mind long since forgotten in a world filled with cement, interstates, jobs, schools and commitments to a society interested in results, material possessions and success. I was being returned to my true home.

Instantaneously, we became the wind. Our spirits soared weightless as we sailed high above the Earth, gazing upon forests, trees, lakes and streams. She and I were indistinguishable. As the spiritual wind moving over the Earth, she contained me. We blew across the sky and I felt a unity about the Earth.

With a flash, we were in space. We gazed upon the Earth below us and she stretched her arms out in an embrace of the entire planet. In imitation of her embrace, I too stretched forth my arms and felt a deep and infinite Love flow through me.

This dream's message was simple and clear to me: *"Embrace life!"* The dream also taught that when you transcend your limited ego and fly in the Spirit, you see the wholeness of life. Perhaps this is the importance of traveling to the mountaintop so prevalent in ancient myth? This would eventually become an important insight for me much later in my life, when I grew to see how all of history (universal, evolutionary, human) is written within each cell of my being. In transcending the individual self by flying into the Spirit, I see the patterns of my life ingrained in the whole of the planet. (See the development of this thought in chapter 6.)

When the woman held out her arms in an embrace of the planet, she was saying, *"I am all this...I am Life."* When I mirrored her embrace, for an instant I too could recognize, *"I am all this!"* In her reappearance after years of what seemed to me to be silence, the woman now confronted me with the essential question facing the seekers of truth throughout the ages: "What is our source of origin?" This question was the great mystery of life. Somehow, the woman appeared to be simultaneously the mystery and the answer. My Soul was on fire. The quest had just begun in my mind. I just had to know who this woman was and why she was reappearing.

Yet, as we have discussed, the woman had never really stopped presenting herself to me; I had simply failed to recognize her. In my spiritual blindness, I was much like the disciples who failed to recognize Jesus after his resurrection, until the Holy Spirit opened their eyes to his identity. In the next chapter, we will focus on how I came to realize her constant availability to me in various forms. We will discover how the occurrence of one powerful mind-altering dream would lead to an integration of the childhood and adult experiences of my friend. In addition we will see how I, just like the hero in *The Neverending Story*, was given the great honor and responsibility of giving my friend a name. In this act, we will also discover how a single dream can lead one humble seeker to the same understanding of the universe that is variously expressed by the world's greatest sages and mystics.

Chapter 3
Naming the Nameless

~

And Moses said unto God, "Behold, when I come unto the children
of Israel and shall say unto them 'The God of your
fathers hath sent me unto you' and they shall say to me,
'What is his name?' what shall I say unto them?"
And God said unto Moses, "I AM THAT I AM" and he said, "Thus shalt
thou say unto the children of Israel, 'I AM has sent me unto you.'"
– Exodus 3: 13-14

Though I had known my mystery friend all my life, her identity remained shrouded. Only the response she elicited in
me was fully evident. Whenever I felt her presence, my emo-
tions would skyrocket into an internal display of ecstatic love.
Her power drove me to my knees in adoration. Her beauty
lifted my Soul. In her, I knew the source of my existence and
all my thoughts. She was the Mother of my life. Whenever I
recognized her presence, Love filled the vacuum of my Soul.

Without knowing it, I was part of a cosmic dance that had
no beginning or end. Deep inside me, a yearning developed to name this woman-friend that had been appearing
since childhood. In a seemingly unconscious way, I was
engaged in the never-ending creative task of the hero, to

give his Empress a name, thereby revealing his own true nature. This personal task that engaged me was universal to the world of myth. As I would soon discover, my friend's manifestations were as varied as there were people in the universe. Yet, she appeared to me, in all her manifestations, as one.

The process of naming the Empress occurs before time while unfolding within time. The importance of naming is highlighted in more than *The Neverending Story*. Even in the Bible's book of Genesis, God is seen naming everything that He brings forth from within himself. It is by his Word that each thing—light, day and night, Earth, seas, creatures and humanity–emerged distinctively from the void. Similarly, he gives Adam the task of naming his Bride, Eve, and each distinct animal. Hence, *The Neverending Story* manifests in the Bible as much as it does in a child's fairy tale. As the story tells, naming is basic to creation. It restores the connection between the namer and the named in much the same way suckling rejoins the infant to its mother.

FOREST DREAM

A pivotal dream strengthened my unconscious drive to name the Empress. Soon after this dream my life began to change:

> *I was taking a leisurely stroll through a quiet and remote wooded area. The sun's rays shone through the trees, reminding me of spotlights on a stage. Flying amongst the trees were several birds. Their melody guided me through the woods, until their bodies lightly came to rest upon the trees' green-leafed branches. They would first fly ahead, come to rest on a branch and then glance back towards me. I found the behavior of these little birds to be curious, while experiencing a deep peace surrounding the entire scene. Everything in this forest connected to one source.*

Coming upon a clearing, I found my childhood friend standing naked in the center of an oval of some short golden grass. This layer of grass then made way to a second oval of longer golden grass, reminding me of wheat.

My eyes were opened to see the many animals that inhabited the forest around her. There were raccoons, a possum, a tiger, hundreds of birds and countless other wild species. The forest just brimmed with life. Directly across from me were two snakes. I glanced at these snakes and noticed they intertwined as they dangled from the limb of a tree. As if to return my gaze, the snakes looked towards me and began darting their tongues.

I re-focused on my friend. A light was striking her from behind, turning her skin a radiant gold. Sparks of light danced joyfully about her hair and body. I felt myself being drawn towards her by the intense power that she radiated. She was like a magnet attracting a nail.

Everything appeared centered on my friend. All the forest creatures looked towards her. She was the source of power for each creature in the forest. Even the trees appeared oriented towards their Mother and reached their mighty arms out to embrace her.

Smiling impishly and with a finger outstretched, my friend addressed me, "And I command you!" As she spoke, I felt her radiance and powers magnify. I discovered I was naked as she moved her hand, with finger still outstretched, to her side. I gazed upon her with the same love and awe I felt for her as a child. I realized she was God. The sense of her presence intensified. This presence was of such intensity that I realized the entire universe emerged from her. She was the center of being for the entire dream.

Upon waking, an intense power circulated throughout my body. My cells erupted with a vibrant energy of incomprehensible magnitude when touched by this power. I knew this power as the woman. She was a river of fire consuming every cell in its path. Yet, it appeared that in this consuming death, I was being reborn.

Words can only attempt to describe the importance of this dream in my life. I have meditated on it for many years and am still inspired by its power and beauty. After this dream, my life was never to be the same, nor was she for she received a name. I began to meditate on the woman as a metaphor for God's Nature and soon gave her a name that had special significance to me.

This dream helped me to understand my visions as a child, my experiences in Nature, and my experiences of emerging from Infinite Being that established the pattern of my life. Those events that before had appeared to be isolated incidents were now evidently intimately connected to each other. My friend's nakedness was a metaphor for the revelation of this pattern. My own nakedness bore witness to my rebirth and indebtedness to her for all the experiences of my life. In revealing herself, she revealed me. She revealed my life's patterns as her creation.

To understand dream symbolism, one needs to correlate the image with the feelings inherent in the dream. The position of my friend and the oval shape of the surrounding grass correspond to the feeling that everything is born of her. The oval of grass signifies feminine genitalia. Like a baby exploding from the body of his mother, the entire cosmos (dream) thundered from the womb of my friend.

The ovular layout of the dream beautifully displays the essence of this process. This layout speaks to the beginning, before the dream unfolds into form. In a metaphorical sense, I was gazing into the place where everything, including myself, existed prior to conception. Through sensing that things emerged from the body of my friend, I was watching my own birth. Indeed, my creation and the dream's creation were one motion generated from her body. I experienced this process in the dream as timeless, occurring here and now and not in the past. The woman was akin to a point from which a fountain of energy gushed forth and became a solid world.

The oval was a popular symbol for the process of birth in ancient cultures. Egyptian scholar, John Anthony West (1993), reflects upon the oval as a metaphor for the open mouth that emits the Word. Since the silence of Nature emitted the "HUM" in my personal experiences (see chapter 2), then Mr. West and I are describing the same thing. If you imagine the oval in the dream, it will be in the shape of a mouth, as well as a vulva. These organs mirror one another.

When the woman said, "And I command *you*," she was saying the dream was her baby and I was a character in it. Like the forest and all its creatures, I flow from the body of my friend. What she speaks becomes. It is not only my dream; it is hers. This insight caused me to go into an epistemological tailspin, for the dream was meditating on its own creation. In watching the dream, I was watching my own birth through metaphorical imagery! In many ways, the thrust of the dream's message was akin to an eye trying to see itself!

The dream imagery reflects the cosmological significance of a woman's body. Women give external form to the internal reality through which conception occurs. The dream reveals that I, as a biological male, have feminine powers within my psyche to give birth to a thought or a dream. Correspondingly, my woman friend has masculine powers to impregnate my thought process. Holistically,

31

male and female, God and Goddess, human and divine are united in the web of Love.

Furthermore, the dream clearly ties into my mystical experiences. The woman was the infinite consciousness out of which I saw my life arise as a light. The woman is the nature of my inner world. She is my Nature. It is interesting that I have always loved nude images. I do not like magazines like *Playboy* or *Hustler*. I find these types of work cheap pornography, reflecting our shallow, sensationalist and commercial society that turns everything, including women, into objects. Yet, I do love nudes and have often thought that artists loved doing images of women because they see the creativity immanent within themselves expressed in the bodies of the women they work with. Just as women conceive babies from within themselves, artists create their works from within. This is why I call this book "my baby." I have labored many years with it and it has come from within myself.

In meditating on this dream in relation to the dream presented in the previous chapter, I recognize a pattern of my imitating her actions. In one dream, like her, I open my arms to the planet, and in this dream, like her, I become naked. What she does, I do. Her embrace is my embrace. Her revelation is my revelation. She and I are one. The microcosm (me) and the macrocosm (my friend) mirror one another. This is the holographic nature of the web.

Hindu writings reflect the holographic composition of the web by saying the Heaven of the God, Indra, contains an infinite number of jewels that mirror every other jewel in that Heaven. We are those jewels. Rudolph Steiner likewise tells us, "*We have within us shadow-images of the great Universe. And all the members of our constitution - the physical, etheric, astral bodies and the ego - are worlds for Divine Beings.*" *(Ibid, p.38)* I believe it is in shadow, only because we are not open to it.

We are the ones who cast "the shadow of doubt" or, indeed, the shroud of denial.

We do not see this mirroring within ourselves because we lock ourselves into a dualistic mode of thinking. Instead of seeing the universe as self, we see it as other. We also tend to compartmentalize everything and, thus, live in "apartments" from Nature. Yet, if we open our eyes, a beautiful mosaic unfolds in such a fashion that all points in our lives mirror each other and serve as a mirror of the universal mosaic.

SYNCHRONICITY

Ultimately, the dream is about a timeless power existing as the epicenter of the universe and explored in both current and ancient teachings. In various ways, the dream spoke to a process that some scientists (e.g., Carl Jung and F. David Peat) call a *synchronicity*. *Synchronicity* refers to a *meaningful coincidence, a significantly related pattern of chance*. Rupert Sheldrake's (1981) theory of *Morphic Resonance* exemplifies synchronicity. This theory proposes that what a particular species learns in one part of the world facilitates similar learning in a comparable species living in another part of the world. It is as if there is an invisible thread connecting animals across the Earth. The animals are not directly in contact with one another. They live in different parts of the world. This simultaneous learning appears to be a meaningful coincidence, a significantly related pattern of chance.

In my view, synchronicity has nothing to do with chance. It is a movement in a particular direction serving in the unfolding of patterns throughout time and space. Synchronicity reveals the universal web. Morphic Resonance is actually a movement in a particular direction. It serves to unfold patterns of behavior in a particular species across the world.

A human example of this process is the simultaneous and independent development of the theory of evolution by Darwin and Wallace in the late 1800's. This simultaneous development of a theory by two different men is a synchronicity. It is the unfolding of a pattern in time and space.

I grew to understand that my dream related to a larger movement occurring across the globe. Before the occurrence of this dream, I had not read anything on the Goddess. However, as if by serendipitous magic, after its occurrence a whole movement of which I had only been dimly aware opened before my eyes. It was as if scales fell from my eyes, revealing a world of Wisdom teachings to which I had previously been blind. Modern archeologists were discovering ancient cultures that were matriarchal in structure and worshipped the Goddess (e.g., Gimbutas, 1982; Graves, 1948). Feminists were questioning how they fit into a predominately male-oriented spirituality (e.g., Walkers, 1983). Men were questioning what they had lost in the suppression of Goddess worship and how it affected our treatment of the environment (e.g., Rozak, 2001). Unearthed writings of Gnostics (Barnstone and Meyer, 2003, Jung, 1976) revealed a strong feminine presence to the deity worshipped by many sects of early Jews and Christians. Other research had uncovered that much of the Bible's writing drew upon ancient matriarchal spirituality (Walkers, 1983). Eco-feminists were questioning how our views of the feminine have led to a destructive and greedy orientation towards Nature (Rozak, 2001). Biologists such as James Lovelock (1995) were expressing theories about the interconnectedness of life on this planet that mirrored the philosophy of ancient Goddess spirituality. Even many quantum physicists reflected the ancient Sea Goddess when they asserted the ground or the universe is an infinite ocean of energy or life (Talbot, 1991).

All of these modern day discoveries corresponded with my dream. Its manifestation in me was an individual expression of an occurrence that was universal. My dream was like a ripple riding a tidal wave, a particular instance of an ongoing global synchronicity. It was an observed particle emerging from the great wave of universal meaning.

Initiating my understanding of how my dream related to a whole movement was the works of psychiatrist, Carl Jung (1976). My first contact with Jung occurred a couple of days after the dream, when I bought a book containing a collection of his writings. I attained these writings in curiosity, seeking theories I could use in my work as a counselor. I received much more, for through Jung I learned of my friend. To my surprise, she blatantly appeared in his writings about the Christian Bible. My first contact with the Christian Goddess occurred in the chapter entitled, "The Structure of the Psyche," (p. 43) where Jung states:

> *Let us take as an example the Christian dogma. The Trinity consists of Father, Son and Holy Ghost, who is represented by the bird of Astarte, the Dove and who in early Christian times was called Sophia and thought of as feminine.*

I read this paragraph over and over. Before this, I had never heard my Sophia mentioned or named by another. I entered a state of shock and disbelief. In all my encounters with Christianity, I had never heard any reference to femininity in God. I immediately recalled the impish smile of the Goddess in the dream. Her smile appeared to mock the view of God taught in church and day-to-day discussions of God in western civilization.

Sophia is a Greek name meaning Wisdom. In meditating on her, I realized she was no different from Siegel's writings on our body's Wisdom in healing (see chapter 2). She was also the Lady of Light envisioned by one client or the Lady dressed in a safari outfit envisioned by another. Since I had equated Nature with Intelligence, it made perfect sense to me that Wisdom manifested as a woman. She was Nature. Everything I had come to believe was right there in Jung's one statement. In these readings, I began to thirst for Sophia. My feeling of being drawn towards my friend, like a nail towards a magnet, was predicting this thirst metaphorically in the dream.

While reading Jung, I felt naked and helpless at the Mother's feet. Sophia had me hook, line and sinker. Like an infatuated lover, I sought her. The more I sought her, the more I found. For example, in Jung's "Answer to Job" (p. 552) I read:

> *"As Ruach, the Spirit of God, she brooded over the waters of the beginning. Like God, she has her throne in Heaven. As the cosmological Pneuma (breath), she pervades and permeates Heaven and Earth and all living things."*

In this paragraph was the message to the dream: *As the Holy Spirit, Sophia is the beginning.* Through these words, my Empress was no longer nameless. Naming her was a sacrament or metaphor for creating her. Thereby, I completed the circle between creature and creator. I am that which turned her into a creator, in the same way that this book creates me as an author or a child recreates a woman as a mother.

NAMING AS CO-CREATING
Naming someone or something is a form of adoration, recognizing and revitalizing the Love from which it emerged, nameless and virgin. God makes the word flesh; we, in turn, sanctify and glorify the flesh by giving it name. This is a heavy concept that we will explore in a different context in

a later discussion of quantum physics. It is also an enlight-ening concept that resolves the enigmatic dualism between creator and creature. My eyes are co-creators with the light from beyond as it is experienced within me.

Personally naming the ineffable generated an awareness of an intimacy that was powerful, beautiful, and yet very frightening. Knowing one's source makes one vulnerable to death of the individual ego. Intimacy can swallow you; make you lose yourself. Yet, it is only in this death that we truly know our eternity. What I find myself fearing is letting go, diving into waters of infinite depths. Yet, in this dream, I was being pushed into doing just that. A mother that loves her son and wants him to learn to swim does that from time to time. She pushes him to jump in.

To summarize, the "Forest Dream" is not just revealing my personal web. It reveals a web that is universal. In its depths, the dream envelops or provides a holograph for all myths, religions and teachings manifesting throughout the variety of human cultures. In its universality, the dream defines a web that ties my personal experiences and dreams to the totality of Nature. The dream's construction mirrors everything else. It is a revelation of Sophia and the beauti-ful web she weaves.

I have since discovered, as I explored the mythology of ancient peoples throughout the world, that she has been given many names: Shakti, Demeter, Athena, Aphrodite, Spider Grandmother, Fate, Destiny, Dana, Isis, Hathor, Marie, Coatilique, Bridget and the Muses among others. My naming of Her, Sophia, is crucial to my claiming of my inherent Soul, just as your naming of her (or him) is crucial to yours. However she is venerated, she is one, Mother of All. In the next chapter, we will take a closer look at the revelation of my personal web and how that web links to all of creation, which, in its diversity, is united as one.

Chapter 4
Revealing the Cosmic Child
〜○

Of what use, Gabriel, is your message to Marie
Unless that message is delivered to me!
~Angelus Silesius

Infinity is infinite in an infinite number of ways. She is infinite in the ways she births us. For example, are we Christian, Muslim, Hindu, Pagan or Jew? Among all the members of these denominations and many more un-named here, do any two believers think exactly alike? Do any two of us look alike? Can any person walk the very same steps as another person? Indeed, can even one person ever walk the same ground twice? Are any two women or men exactly alike? Is any woman or man exactly as (s)he was yesterday? No! Everything changes. Change is the only thing of which we can be certain. Such is the paradox of the universe that envelops us, for it is the manifestation of infinite potential.

Not realizing the infinity of perspectives, we often squelch creative diversity within our institutional religions and political systems. A person who questions doctrine is often excommunicated, deemed a heretic, branded as evil, put to death or tortured. His or her family is put through hell. A citizen who opposes war policies is branded as one who aids and abets the "enemy" and endangers the troops. Even our current culture is about regimenting the individual. For example, in preparing children for industry and military through schools, we teach them to line up, shut up, sit up straight and do as you're told! Schools are not based upon the educational philosophies of Thomas Dewey, as stated. They are based on the assembly line theories of Henry Ford! The objective of the school system is to manufacture products that will be profitable to the government, industry, and the military. Our educational system is not geared towards helping an individual unfold his potential.

When will we let go and allow the true potential of all persons to unfold? This control and domination ethos, reflected in regimentation, exists not only in the system's relationship to its subjects. The same ethos is also in our heads. How often do we badger ourselves for not being perfect? What is *perfect* except *conforming to an externally imposed model?* How many young girls become anorexic or bulimic because they are brainwashed into believing they have to have the "perfect" bodies defined by commercial propaganda? Why can't they allow their *true* beauty to unfold? Why can't all girls be recognized for what they are: goddesses, the beginning and end of all things? How many men miss the richness of a full relationship because they cannot allow themselves to feel and, instead, think they must be in control at all times? Why can't they allow themselves the vulnerable richness of emotional depth? Why can't men be recognized for what they are: gods, the passionate Eros of creation?

We don't trust ourselves, because we don't trust Nature's process, i.e., Sophia. When we see our creation and ourselves as separate from the natural evolution ordained by

Wisdom, we separate ourselves from our true identity and the Earth that sustains us. We fail to see that evolution *IS* Nature's intelligent design. We doom ourselves to irreconcilable alienation, becoming strangers in a strange and hostile land. We consign ourselves to the perpetual insecurity that necessitates warfare. Our inner and outer warfare is reflected in our domination and control of Nature. What we do internally is what we do externally. We don't allow Nature to unfold and we don't allow ourselves to unfold. In our patriarchy, the emphasis is on regimentation, as in the army, and not on questioning the authorities or the status quo.

My personal task–and I believe it to be the task of all of humans–is to allow the Self or Nature to unfold. It is my view that when this Self is known within us, then we can proclaim that the Christ, the Buddha, or the Divine Child has been reborn into the world. This Self has been suppressed within the world and within ourselves.

Yet, his/her birth is all of our stories. Each of our lives is the process of enfolding and unfolding Truth and Love. While there are an infinite number of stories, there is just one. Just as Lord Jesus went into hiding with his Mother for fear of King Herod destroying him in his infancy, we have gone into hiding, masquerading as people other than who we are in our naked essence. In that nakedness we are God. Why else would the status quo look at nudity in such disdain? They can't handle the glory of the naked Truth, which is what we are in our true Nature. Look at how naked the crucified Christ is in medieval art and how powerfully beautiful he is in that nakedness.

To be reborn as the Cosmic Person and reveal the naked beauty of our Self, we need to reenter the womb of Sophia. With Love she entices us inward so that we may dissolve and be reborn. As Rumi says:

A new moon teaches gradualness
and deliberation and how one gives birth
to oneself slowly. Patience with small details
makes perfect a large work, like the universe.

What nine months of attention does for an embryo
Forty early mornings will do
For your gradually growing wholeness.
(1997, p. 49)

DREAM: GHOST OF LOST FRIEND

Just as we enter the dark void of sleep each night to be reborn in the morning, we must enter the dark depths of our Souls, which comprise the Mother's body. The process is one that frightens us. That fear was immanent in the following dream I had in the early 80s:

I was at a party where I was looking for a girl that I was in love with. I was standing, having a drink, and talking with her father. I stated that I did not know where she was and felt afraid for her. I then felt a cold chill I realized as a ghost. Another man that I was with stated, "Ghosts are things that are dead but come back to haunt us. They really aren't dead at all."

The father and I were in a basement tunnel composed of dirt, under the house. We continued looking for the girl. I felt very afraid for her as I felt the cold air intensify.

I was then in the parlor of the house. I gazed outside through a picture bay window that had a chest as its base. I noticed a large tree outside in the yard. The tree was barren of leaves. I felt a cold chill in the air and went outside to escape. I knew the air was the girl's ghost. The air became colder and began to whirl around me. I stated three times, "I care for the girl; I am powerless. There's nothing I can do." The wind began to blow colder with each time I spoke these words. I wanted to run but realized I would be followed by this ghost wherever I went.

A ghost is something of the past that continues to emerge in our minds as memories. As if to go into the memory, I go with the girl's father in a basement tunnel, under the house. We had gone underground, reflecting that we were in the belly or womb of the Earth. Being a tunnel reflected it as being a passage, like a birth canal. To what did I need to be reborn?

I then found myself in the parlor of the house with a wide picture-bay window opening onto a view of the yard with a large tree. I felt the girl's ghost. But, I was powerless to love her. Ghosts are things that are dead, but really aren't dead at all. They are memories stored in our psyche. What is the memory haunting me? What did I need to be able to love again?

The ghost that haunted me was revealed in another dream that followed:

I was alone in a white house that had been the setting for many of my previous dreams. Warm air blew through a window to my right and I felt embraced by it. I gazed forward, towards a bay window that had a treasure chest as its base. Outside was the familiar tree, still in bloom. Sitting upon the chest naked was Sophia, with her right foot elevated on top of the chest and her left foot dangling to the floor. As she noticed me, she smiled teasingly and opened her legs slightly saying, "Be as you were in the beginning."

This dream's message is to go inward, into the Goddess. Only so could I love fully what had eluded me as the cold wind of the previous dream. As revealed in the last chapter, the Goddess I named Sophia *is* my inner reality, my creative power. It was She that I was destined to love.

When I think of my relationship to women as lover and son, I think of this process as being revealed in the Star of David. The downward pointing triangle is the movement of birth into the world. The upward pointing triangle is the movement back into the "Promised Land." For me, this Promised Land is the return to Sophia, i.e., the dark cosmic womb of Infinity that I hold within myself and, in which, God sits in all his glory.

Interestingly, the original name for the Goddess Isis in Egypt was *Au-Set,* meaning *Throne of Power.* It was upon her lap that the God was said to sit and derive his kingship. This story became the impetus for placing such high importance on thrones in our past history, for it was upon the throne, i.e., the Goddess, that the king derived his power.

This same concept is reflected in Hindu where the feminine *Shakti* is said to be the Creative Power of God, whom the masculine *Shiva* manifests, however imperfectly, in his drunken, boastful unfaithfulness. In psychoanalytic psychiatry, this reflects the so-called *unconscious* that serves as the base for the *conscious* mind. (I say "so-called" because the *unconscious* is *more* conscious than our so-called *conscious.* While this ego "I" has no idea on how to build a body, my cells do have the knowledge and execute it quite well. Even science is still at the hypothesis stage regarding this process.)

My invitation into this inward process is reflected in Sophia's call to enter into her and become united with God, as I was in the Beginning. This call is actually into death but it is through this death that a new life will unfold within me. Hence, the dream is a call to die in her. The upward movement of the Star of David speaks to this process and is reflected in the act of intercourse. At birth our movement is down and out. During intercourse, it is up and in. Going inward is movement upwards, towards transcendence or wholeness. What is intercourse if not a desire to unite and become part of the whole? What is true between our legs is true in the movement of our Soul, for in this spiritual process we die to our individual self and see the wholeness of our life. We reunite with the Beloved.

SPIRALS

As a child I unconsciously realized this process. Ever since I can remember, I have always drawn spirals. They call to me and I am entranced by them. My three-year-old grand-daughter also draws them repeatedly. Apparently, they are a symbol important to the collective unconscious. Ancient matriarchal societies drew spirals all the time (see Gimbutas, 1982). The spiral was also said to move clockwise to represent entrance into the world and counterclockwise to represent death or return to the central point. This idea was so powerful that the patriarchs tried to get control of the peasant matriarchal societies they invaded by deeming even dancing in a counterclockwise fashion to be evil, to be dealt with by heavy consequences (Walker, 1983).

The process of dying and being born again is also the process of our revelation. Even the Bible's Book of Revelations begins with much violence and destruction before the new world in the form of New Jerusalem, the *place of peace,* descends to her groom. Likewise, for deeper understanding of the cosmos and ourselves, we have to take the axe to what we think we know. We have to destroy the status quo and allow Sophia's creativity to flow from within. Revelations is not really about a time in the future. It reveals a process in the eternal now. Our hiding our true selves is the hiding of the Woman with 12 stars above her head hiding her infant from the tyranny of the 7-headed monster. To uncover ourselves as the Cosmic Man is to be born again into Peace or Jerusalem. To do so, we have to descend into our inward depths; only from there can we ascend the heights. Within time, we will unfold ourselves as the manifestation of God. We will know ourselves as Adamah (Adam), made in the image of God, male and female (Genesis 1:27).

Adam is often seen as the fallen man with Christ being the one who ascends back into Heaven. Christ, in other words, is often seen as the second Adam. Yet, I say there are not two Adams. There is one Adam that is both "fallen" and "resurrected." This does not mean that we should view our Earthly life with disdain. Indeed, our Earth is the womb that will allow us to unfold our potential of being resurrected into timeless life. In the final vision we will find ourselves in the dark depths of Sophia's womb, the timeless and spaceless expanse of Infinity.

In writing the following poem, I found that womb as one with Gaia, or Earth:

> *Truth unfurls within you, Cosmic Girl*
> *Inward you must journey towards your Source*
>
> *Deny external teachers claiming to know all*
> *Dive deep where you shall meet a stranger of sorts*
> *For it is none other than I AM behind the call*
>
> *Find home within your heart*
> *Give birth to the Eternal "OM"*
> *The world forms from this sacred sound*
> *Your being explodes from this timeless realm.*

VISION: INSIDE THE WEB

As my poem implies, the Cosmic Man and Woman envelops the entire universe, including us. For example, in a vision, I saw my life laid out as a web spun by Sophia.

My brain and every cell of my body were connected by invisible threads of light. My brain, in turn, was a mirror to the web of invisible lights connecting the entire universe. This web reached into the farthest reaches of Heaven and Earth. There was nowhere I was not. From there, I saw that my body spun itself into past and future history. There was no time in which I was not. In seeing this web, I had a deep sense of my ancestry and realized what appeared dead and gone were alive and quite well in me. My body was the unfolding of information from centuries in the past, even before human beings came into being. I was the Amoeba arising from the primordial muck.

I then saw the weave as spanning all peoples and indeed the entire future history of Earth. I saw how wise our ancestors were in planning for the effects of current decisions on their posterity seven generations hence. I saw that just as my ancestors live on in me, so also do I live on in my descendants. Moreover, the very energies inherent in my life will return to Nature and be woven into a multitude of life forms. All our choices co-create one reality. Together we manifest heaven and/or hell on Earth.

This Earthly movement then transcended itself and I saw the web in the spiritual heavens and within all dimensions of beings. There was nowhere my web had not been or will not be. I was infinite and eternal. I was what I loved most. I was the Son of Sophia as well as Sophia herself.

This vision speaks against the common sense notion of our being finite beings living and dying in a finite world. In our dualistic, "either/or" mentality, we see ourselves as separate from the infinite. Yet, we are both finite and infinite (Earth and Heaven) for Sophia is able to think in terms of "both-and" in addition to the "either/or" mentality characteristic of modern thought processes.

BOTH-AND

In a group exercise at a retreat, my supervisor did an abstract clay image that illustrates the "both/and" mindset beautifully. The base of this image looked like a tree trunk with the top being a lot of serpentine figures snaking their way into space. Nestled within these serpentine arms were what appeared to be eggs or rocks. As I saw the image, I recognized Sophia's hand at work, for this sculpture conveyed the notion of our being both quietly at peace and noisily aggressive. While the serpentine figures appeared to be moving in frenetic disarray, they were anchored in a tree trunk that appeared still, peaceful and unmoving. In addition, nestled among the serpents, were a lot of little eggs that spoke to me as potentials.

In my reading of the message of the clay image, we are finite, as expressed by the multitude of moving serpentine figures, and also infinite, as represented in the peaceful, unmoving tree trunk. As I meditated upon the artwork, I saw that we are simultaneously leading busy lives and being anchored in peace. Proverbs: 3:17 states that the paths of Sophia are peace. Carl Jung (1976) in some of his writings links her to Jerusalem, which literally means, "Place of Peace." While we live in an unsettling world in an unsettled mind, our foundation is Peace. Jerusalem is here now, existing as the stillness in the midst of turmoil. She is the page upon which the word is written. She is the silence surrounding and defining the words we speak. This is the message I received in response to my supervisor's image. It is the message of Sophia.

In our depths we are filled with infinite Wisdom. As much as I realize myself as a manifestation of the Divine Child, I recognize in the supervisor who created this image another manifestation of the same Child, expressed in a unique way. What is the name for the Child in my supervisor's world? Whatever speaks to her heart! In the final analysis, we each have the task to give our Empress a name. Just as all colors, blended together, form white; so all our names for her, spoken together, will, I believe, form the ineffable Om, Hum, "Light murmuring sound" or song of the stars discussed in chapter two. Each of our individual voices is crucial to manifesting the divine music of her true unspeakable name. We are all essential to the totality of the chorus.

It is we, her sons and daughters, who bequeath her the divine title: MOTHER. Were it not for us, that part of her holiness would not be manifest, remaining forever the unfertilized eggs, the unrealized potential. Yet the eternal, infinite one cannot be incomplete. Ergo: We are inevitable! That is how important our divine task of naming her truly is!

Part 2:

Lifting Sophia's Veil

Chapter 5
The Web of Life

Every body placed in the luminous air spreads out in circles
and fills the surrounding space with infinite likeness of itself
and appears all in all and all in every part.
~ Leonardo da Vinci

*W*hen Sophia took me above the Earth (chapter 2), I saw how transcending my orientation on the planet led to a picture of the planet in her wholeness. As I grew older, I discovered this message was multidimensional in its implications. For example, there is this particular hill on Route 4 in Turner, Maine that I am particularly attracted to. Just because of the exposed rock face, I named this hill "Baldy." From my up-close, on-the-ground perspective, I saw the hill as being an individual existing independent of the rest of the scenery.

However, when I saw that same hill from Rt. 106, which is further away to the east and somewhat elevated, I saw it as being part of a pattern that contained other hills. It was as if the hill was part of a series of wrinkles in a bed sheet. I began to generalize this lesson. Seeing this hill as part of a pattern enabled me to learn about other parts of my life.

When I was able to get beyond myself, as metaphorically represented by my flying with Sophia, I saw myself as part of a web that included everything within this universe. Instead of an isolated person, I was part of an interwoven pattern of life that included all things. Conversely, the entire pattern existed within me.

In the days of the ancients, the Goddess was said to be the weaver of life. Whether she was the southwestern Native American Spider Grandmother spinning her web, the Greek Fates weaving destiny, or the Hindu Kali spinning the universe from her own substance, the Goddess was said to weave everything together as a woman weaves an article of clothing. Just as the mountains revealed from above showed me a great tapestry, our Mother has long been known as the creator of a great tapestry. As we will see in this chapter, it now appears the ancients had it right all along. We live in a wondrous web where every event does not exist discretely, but is a part of the web's tapestry.

My dreams taught me an important lesson: *everything is part of this great web of life.* As I meditated on the Goddess, I furthermore found that we are more than a part of the web. We are the web's totality! I know this claim sounds outrageous to the uninitiated, but bear with me and you will see its truth.

To understand that this mind-boggling notion is not so farfetched, consider molecular biology. According to this field of inquiry, there is a molecule, called DNA, contained in each cell of our body. This DNA molecule instructs each cell how to function and form. For example, the DNA of a brain cell instructs that cell how to form and function as a brain cell. Each molecule of DNA contains much more information than the instructions for the particular cell it commands. Indeed, each molecule contains knowledge for every one of the distinctive cells in the body. For example, the DNA of a brain cell contains information regarding the functioning of a heart, a liver and a hand. Each cell in our body ultimately contains knowledge for making a complete person. The instructions for making a particular kind of cell are "turned on" through complex interactions between all the cells of the body. Cells essentially talk to each other in determining how they will manifest within the developing embryo. A particular cell manifests because of its relationship to the whole.

SCIENTISTS AND MYSTICS ON THE WEB OF LIFE

I am not the first to have observed that this phenomenon pervades nature. Physicist David Bohm, describes the universe as a multidimensional web constructed in such a way that each dimension of the web reflects and contains every other dimension holographically (Bohm, 2002). Every person reading this book reflects and contains every blade of grass, every cloud, every planet in our solar system and every star in the universe in his or her own unique way. For example, our circulatory system, composed of heart, arteries and veins, reflects and is another manifestation of the circulatory system of the Earth, composed of oceans, atmosphere, rivers and streams. Similarly, our brains contain billions of neurons firing and making connections, just as the dark, spacious depths of the Milky Way contain billions of stars firing and connecting.

What we see outside is what we see inside. We are a mind nestled within Mind. We–along with everything else--are holographic reflections of the entire universe. The universe both unfolds and enfolds itself as unique forms in such a way that everything mirrors, reflects and contains everything else. Every blade of grass, every woman, every man, every cloud in the sky is the All expressed as a part and each of these parts contains and mirrors the All.

St. Hildegard of Bingen reflects this same idea from a spiritual and cosmological point of view when she states, *"God creates everything with everything else in mind"* (Fox, 1998, p. 19). The macroscopic is fully contained in the microscopic. Goethe even breaks down the distinction between fact and theory: *"All fact is really theory. The blue of the sky reveals to us the basic law of color. Search nothing beyond the phenomena, they themselves are the theory."* (Goethe, *Theory of Colours*, paragraph #50.)

Even more miraculous, according to Carl Sagan (1980), each DNA molecule contains knowledge regarding the entire evolutionary development of our species and ultimately the entire planet. If you ever see photos of a developing fetus, you will notice it will, at various points in its development, look like a fish, a snail, a koala bear and even a snake. This reveals the fact that all creatures are within us. Every one of our cells recapitulates the entire evolutionary history of our planet. The DNA molecule is a hidden totality. In any particular cell, one aspect of that totality has unfolded and manifested.

This containment of all evolutionary history in a single person eventually transcends the biological development of life on Earth. It literally reaches into the depths of the universe. The more we dive into ourselves, the more universal we become. As physicists such as David Bohm (Talbot, 1981) and medical practitioners such as Deepak Chopra (1993) have reflected, our bodies are more than 99.999% empty space. We are not solid at all! The atoms and molecules dancing throughout our bodies are energy trails proportionately as void as intergalactic space. Inner space and outer space are not two! If you want to see what you really look like, gaze into the nighttime sky. You are an expression of the entire cosmos. Conversely, the entirety of the universe that you contemplate exists in your eyes. Like the DNA molecule, you are both a hidden totality and also a singularity in creative relationship with all the other participants in our Universe, past, present and future.

QUANTUM PHYSICS

This conception gets even more exciting as we explore Quantum Physics. The behavior of electrons has long baffled scientists in this field, because electrons appear as waves when not being observed and as particles when being observed. It seems that the very act of observing an electron makes information about that electron manifest in the field of time and space. When not being observed, the electron spreads out and behaves like a wave. It even appears to be at two places at once! According to physicist David Bohm, this odd behavior of an electron means it is not one thing, but a hidden totality or ensemble, enfolded throughout the whole of space (see Talbot, 1981, p. 47). When a scientific instrument *detects* (observes) the presence of an electron, it is because one aspect of the electron's ensemble has unfolded in response to the observation. The movie, *What the Bleep Do We Know!?*, explores this creative transaction between observer and observed. (Arntz, Chasse, and Vicente) This holistic process immanent in the electron *mirrors* the process immanent in DNA. DNA is an ensemble of codes containing the entire evolutionary development of humanity and the knowledge of every cell in a person's body. An electron, as a wave, is a hidden totality enfolded throughout the universe!

POETS AND ARTISTS ON HOLISM

To put it more poetically, consider the words of the great poet and mystic, William Blake (Briggs and Peat, p. 112):

> *To see the World in a grain of sand,*
> *and Heaven in a wildflower.*

Hold Infinity in the palm of your hand,
and Eternity in an hour.

Another great poet, E. E. Cummings, expresses the miraculous paradox this way:

For whatever we lose (like a you or a me)
It's always ourselves we find in the sea

Just listen to Leonardo da Vinci whose quotation is the header for this chapter! These artistic geniuses realized the holographic nature of Nature long before scientists observed the phenomenon. As the saying goes, "All roads lead to Rome." All threads in the great Web of Life lead to the Home in which we are dialectically embedded. She who is in Oz is simultaneously in Kansas!

Goethe foreshadows this understanding of the holographic essence of Nature in his discussion of light. "He sees tension and its reconciliation as prime forces in nature that can be discovered in countless ways. Light and darkness, colors and their complements, colored objects seen and the resulting after-images, seeing and thing seen, person and world–all point toward an instantaneous, living dialectic that joins the parts in a dynamic, interpenetrating whole. This relationship, says the philosopher Eric Heller, is *"a creative conversation between within and without, a kind of dialectical education through which the individual form becomes in actuality what from the very beginning it had been potentially. For what is within and what is without are…merely poles of one and the same thing."* (Seaman, 1998) Goethe wished us to discover how all parts of nature, including ourselves, are integrated, belonging to one Nature.

As a part, we are whole. Heaven and Earth are within us, just as they are in a wildflower and a grain of sand. Being eternally complete and whole, there is no progress or evolution. We evolve in this world to realize and manifest what we already are. Our realization of Truth is but the recognition of what has always been and always will be. The so-called "fall into duality" that many spiritually minded people discuss is but a forgetting of who we have always been. It is a forgetting (albeit a six thousand year long forgetting!) of our wholeness. Our life's task is to remember and fully manifest who we are.

RE-MEMBERING WHO WE ARE

To remember who we are is to re-member. It is to reintegrate ourselves. We are not separate from who the cosmos is. This knowledge of ourselves as wholeness, mirroring the All, is within us as a potential insight, awaiting that ripe, fertilizing moment to unfold. When we become receptive observers, ready to attend to the magnitude of our identity with All, voila! That which was an indefinite wave will be particularly clear.

I hope this section of *Sophia's Web* will be one of the initiators of that insight within you. I hope the fertile seed of thought will gestate within you and transform your life. When we start seeing our relation to all of history, every woman and man, every myth and legend ever told, and every star in the sky, then knowledge of our wholeness is starting to unfold. Ultimately, this knowledge leads to our knowledge of our unity with God and the Goddess that even now is weaving our lives into the creation of an infinite spectrum of universes. Every now and then, we receive a glimpse of this hidden knowledge. These glimpses are the mystical experiences, insights, and dreams we may experience from time to time.

The teachings of the world's great sages, mystics, and intellectuals exist in their fullness within you. You recognize their manifestation of Truth and they appear beautiful for you. Their ideas "come home" to you. You contain the stories of scripture, even as the stories of scripture contain you. Their words are just sound waves in space or wiggles on a page until your receptive mind recreates their meaning. They are only wise if they resonate with a touchstone of Truth within you, so that you recognize (re-cognize) their wisdom. These hidden and unborn spiritual insights wait in patience for those ripe and fertile times to erupt from our psychic wombs so they can dance majestically before us. Insight into the universe is "in–sight." It is seeing within yourself. By the powers of insight, you can discover how you connect. You can learn not only how you are related to other people, but to everything. Just as an electron and DNA enfold a hidden totality; so do you. Knowing this, you can discover your eternal Nature. I cannot teach you this. Only if my words ring true to your heart will you digest them and create your own insight into the matter. Otherwise, you will blow them off as absurd.

In the next chapter, we will take this idea further and explore the holographic universe more fully. Through this knowledge, we will begin to take an axe to our alienation and begin living in a universe that is.

Chapter 6
Mirror, Mirror in Us All
❧

O' wonderful Mahamaya,
who can analyze your dream power,
projecting with each second the momentary universe?
O' Goddess eternally mad with Bliss,
why have you driven us mad
with habitual diversion!
~ Ramprasad (Hixon, 1994, p. 110)

*I*n today's world, we pit one thing against the other. This is true in politics, religion, science and our families. It is even true within ourselves. For example, a Muslim may cry, "There is no God but Allah" and attack all other Gods as "wrong." Likewise, a conservative Christian might cry out that Jesus is the only Way and that Muslims and everybody else are lost in sin. On a political front, a conservative Republican might attack a liberal Democrat as the greatest threat to our nation, while the Democrat is saying the same about the Republican.

While these various viewpoints are attacking one another, they are inextricably linked by a fundamental shared belief: *their* way is *the only true* way. "It's my way or the highway!"

They are blind to their ultimate worship of one false god: their own arrogant cognition. Along with that mindset comes the justification of violence, necessary to confront a perceived threat from the other and convert him to the one right way. While a conservative Christian President can get up and spout the words of Jesus, "Do not remove the smite from thy brother's eye unless you remove it from your own," the fact is he is unable to see in his brother's eye his own desire to control and dominate for political, financial, and personal ambitions. In his self-centered arrogance, the President cannot see himself reflected in those he wars against, i.e., the terrorists. Yet, it is terrorism that he himself is condoning by bombing innocent civilians and allowing for torture in the prisons housing those that he thinks are against him. "Shock and Awe" is a whitewashing of the black evil we deem "terrorism." George Bush, Barack Obama and Osama Bin Laden failed to see each other in the mirror only because they see through lenses of a good/evil dichotomy.

REPLACING A MINDSET OF VIOLENCE

Our hope for peace can only be conceived by a fertilizing awakening to this kind of mirroring. We are related to everybody and everything we take in through our senses. From the instant we perceive them, they become an embedded part of us. We are not only what we eat, but what we see, hear, smell, taste, and touch as we "digest" these things according to our values and experience. Does some aspect of somebody else particularly distress you? Look within your own heart. It must be an issue for you, too, or it would not resonate so strongly.

Just as a brother and sister may look something like mom and dad and hence like each other, we all can see our God and Nature reflected in everyone else's eyes and in the essence of their being, including their religious practices (or lack thereof). We don't any longer need to live in an "either–or" dichotomy. We can now choose "both–and."

But whoa! I, too, am setting up another dichotomy, even as I write this. I am falling for the same fallacy, setting up "both-and" as superior to "either-or." I have unwittingly presented my reader with another "either-or" proposition. Even this, too, needs to be transcended. Perhaps this could mean that the true answer to the universe is a great big "Yes!" to all perspectives. (Oh, how my acculturated mind wants to argue, "Yes, BUT...some perspectives are more accurate than others!" Hierarchical thinking is pandemic in our dualistic, patriarchal cultures. It is the crutch upon which dualism leans. However, God/Goddess apparently says "Yes" to all perspectives, allowing the tares to grow alongside the wheat and the Hitlers alongside the Gandhis. Should I second-guess Divine Wisdom?) Such a transformative mindset is seminal if we are to give birth to a culture of peace.

For example, some Christians believe that the idea of "the Word made flesh" as their Jesus is an idea unique to their religion and that makes their religion true. Yet, the idea of the world as a word, a dream or a thought exists throughout the various cultures of humanity. Illustrating the universality of this idea is the Australian Aborigine's *All Mother* giving birth to *dreamtime.* It also manifests in the Keres Pueblo's *Thinking Woman,* who generates everything by her thoughts. Genesis illuminates this idea every time God speaks, "Let there be..." and something new becomes. Regardless of culture, the message is the same: The universe, in all its glories and tribulations, is a dream, a thought or a word arising from the Infinite. All that is flows from the dark, mysterious lips of Sophia, Divine Wisdom. She may be called by many names and still remain One, whole and inviolate. She apparently speaks one Truth in many languages. Every rock, every hill, every culture, every individual has a unique way of revealing the All-in-all. What changes is the wording.

LINGUISTICS AND LOGIC

While scientists tend to use linear logic, spiritual teachers tend toward another vocabulary and structure, and artists towards a third. Yet all pursue Truth. This chapter relates the three in a rather scholarly way. For some readers, such detailed scholarship may be confusing and annoying. They may want to skim or skip this and can do so with my blessings. For other readers, this scholarship may be illuminating and confirming. They may experience this as crucial to my whole thesis. Blessings to them, too!

Brian Steemsa (2006), a mathematician engaged in chaos theory, gets at the abovementioned insight regarding the transformation in mindset needed to steer the world away from its current, self-destructive path when he says:

> *In today's reality of corporate sponsored mental slavery, would-be fascist world dictators (G.W. BUSH) and widespread environmental/ecological disaster areas, it seems that we, the human species, have reached a critical point in our evolution. It's already too late in the day to solve our problems by phasing out hydrocarbon based fuels, by reorganizing the world's financial and governmental institutions or by engineering more advanced versions of the assembly line. What we need is a shift in planetary consciousness, an explosion of radiant conscious energy which can reshape our entire perception of the universe in a single instant of NOW. All we need is Love. All we need is Love. All we need is Love.*
>
> *(GaianXaos)*

64

In modern times, we separate dreams from the surface world. We refer to the former as unreal and the latter as real. Yet, when dreaming, the dream seems as real to us as the world seems in waking life. Perhaps the world of dreams and the waking world are simply different *loci* on the full spectrum of our consciousness or Soul? Think of a rainbow. A rainbow is a spectrum of colors generated by the shattering of sunlight. The sun's light contains all colors and is fragmented into its components by the action of rain or a prism. It would be an illusion for us to think the orange of the rainbow is less real or valid than the yellow. Both are components of the sun's light. It is the same thing with dreams and waking consciousness. They are states of the Soul that ultimately are not distinct. The metaphorical language of dreams and the language of our waking world are not two. Could we also say that the various religions of the world are just different strands of the same rainbow, different dreams of one Dreamer?

TRADITIONAL AND METAPHORICAL LOGIC
We make a similar mistake of fragmenting life when we separate logic from metaphor. In today's world, logic is *the way* of communicating, while metaphor equates with myth and is treated as untrue. Hierarchy places logic above metaphor. However, Matthew Fox (1981, p. 97) considers metaphor God's language, while epistemologist Gregory Bateson (1985) considers metaphor Nature's language. In my view, Nature and God are not two for–as the forest dream of chapter 3 taught me–Sophia is my nature or essence. Bateson contrasts traditional logic with metaphorical logic below (Capra, 1981, p. 81):

Traditional Logic	*Metaphorical Logic*
Men die	*Men die*
Socrates is a man	*Grass dies*
Socrates will die	*Men are grass*

The column headed *Traditional Logic* is known as a Socratic syllogism. This type of logic concerns itself with classifications that establish class membership by identification of subjects or nominatives. The Socratic syllogism identifies items or things (Socrates is a man). This type of logic is not without its faults. Suppose we came across a syllogism such as:

Socrates says, "All Greeks are liars."
Socrates is a Greek.

What conclusion can we make? If we say, "Socrates is a liar", then our preposition becomes "not all Greeks are liars" because Socrates is a liar about Greeks being liars. This means Socrates might be telling the truth. If Socrates is telling the truth that all Greeks are liars, then he is lying. If he is a liar, then he is lying about all Greeks being liars. He could be telling the truth. We could go on and on with this. Forever! Plug this into your multi-megabyte computer and see how long it takes before it blows up.

In contrast to Socratic Logic, metaphorical logic arrives at a truth by identifying verbs or predicates ("Men die – Grass dies"). According to Bateson, metaphor expresses structural similarity or similarity of organization. In my words, metaphor describes functional similarity. For example, how are mulch, the sun's rays, and male sexuality similar? Woman—be she Mother Earth or a human woman–absorbs them in conceiving new life! Our conditioned minds, educated in the linear logic of Socrates, reject the "Men are grass" conclusion as absurd. Reconsider this statement in the light of a holographic analysis, however. We *are* grass, just as we are everything else that lives and dies. We *are* metaphorical beings or holographic expressions of the whole. Jesus' admonition, "Remember, O Man, that you are dust," depends on metaphorical logic. It requires a mindset that accepts the deeper truth exposed by metaphor, making the "Men are grass" syllogism more comprehensible.

One of Bateson's main aims in his study of epistemology, which he defined as *what it's all about*, was to point out that Socratic logic is unsuitable for describing biological patterns. According to Bateson, such logic is fine for linear cause and effect relationships. However, when sequences become circular or cyclical, as they do in the living world, their description in linear terms generates paradoxes. In other words, you get a circular "Yes, but..." type of conclusion such as the quandary illustrated in Socrates' statement of all Greeks being liars.

Our ancestors swam in metaphorical language. It was the language of their rituals and myth and remains the language of today's rituals. For example, what is church communion other than the absorption of the Word so we can become filled (i.e., pregnant) with him? The sacrament of wine simultaneously *being* blood and bread *being* the body of Christ requires a suspension of linear logic in favor of the deeper metaphorical logic that underlies all meaning. Metaphor is verbal sacrament, connecting heaven to earth.

Metaphorical logic is a *pattern that connects*. Our "unconscious minds" fully recognize, absorb, and realize these connecting patterns. To the "unconscious," it does not matter what is absorbed. What is important is the connecting pattern between events and not the thing in question. Absorption leads to conception that leads to birth. This is natural law. Human sexuality is but one mirroring manifestation of that law.

METAPHORICAL SIGNIFICANCE OF SEXUALITY

This process of sexuality mirroring universal process provides an example of the holographic theories of physicist, David Bohm. (See Talbot, 1991 for an easy-to-read introduction to Bohm.) Originally, Bohm was one of the disciples of Albert Einstein. In contemplating many of the findings of physics, he eventually moved beyond Einstein's thoughts and was inspired by the art of holography in creating a model of the cosmos. This model helped him explain many of the paradoxes of quantum physics. For example, his work helped explain why two photons (the most basic unit of matter yet discovered by humans) changed simultaneously upon an experimental manipulation of only one of the photons. It did not matter how far apart these photons were; when one changed, the other would change simultaneously. For this type of phenomena to occur, the signals of the photons would have to be moving at speeds exceeding the speed of light. According to the laws of traditional physics, this notion was absurd. For this type of event to occur, the universe would have to be composed of infinite mass.

Mass, as Einstein's $E=mc^2$ reflects, is energy. As such, Bohm states the world we perceive is only a tiny fragment of reality. He calls our perceived reality the *unfolded* or *manifest explicit order*. Our perceptions of this explicit order have emerged as special forms from a much larger matrix that he refers to as the *enfolded* or *unmanifest implicate order*. This implicate order is an *infinite ocean of energy* (infinite mass, the Alma Mater) emphasizing the wholeness of the whole and the wholeness of the part. That which we perceive as reality is like a projected holographic image arising from this ocean.

In the movie, *What the Bleep Do We Know!?*, this unmanifest is spoken of as a sea of infinite potential or possibilities. (Arntz, Chasse, & Vincente) What manifests out of these possibilities is determined by a functional relationship between consciousness and the pattern of waves upon the ocean. Similarly, Wolf (2001) identifies consciousness as primal in the determination of what manifests by relating the hologram to the ancient concept of the spider's web. A web, he explains, is made of vibrating threads while a hologram is made of vibrating (waves) light. Just as sunlight contains all the colors of the rainbow (even the ones invisible to the human eye), the hologram contains all the possibilities that are made explicit by the observer.

BOHM, PRIBRAM, AND THE HOLOMOVEMENT

Bohm describes the unmanifest as an unbroken whole involved in an unending process of change. This process of change is called the *holomovement*. Herein lies the mystery we call "life". The holomovement is an unfolding of patterns in time and space. It is a movement in a particular direction and corresponds to the process of synchronicity described by Jung (1976).

To understand Bohm's theories, let's take a quick look at how an artist creates a holograph (Talbot, 1991). When an artist creates a holographic image, part of the process is in the recording of a target image, such as an apple, on a holographic plate. This plate contains wave-like interference patterns and appears as water appears in a bathtub after a person swirls it around for a while. When shining a laser through these patterns, a three-dimensional image of the apple appears. An interesting event occurs if we take our holographic plate and cut it in half. Upon dissection, each half of the plate contains an image of the entire apple. Even if we continue to divide the holographic plate into smaller and smaller pieces, we will always get a whole apple. Never do we get a partial apple, though the images we do get may become more "fuzzy" as we continue to divide. What this means is that *the image encoded in each part of the holographic plate is a hidden totality enfolded throughout the whole plate.*

Mirroring this idea is the Hamilton-Jacobi theory of quantum physics (Peat, 1987). According to these theorists, the world is a dance of interacting waves. Motion emerges out of the whole complex movement of these waves. Individual movement is similar to a little boat being tossed and moved about by the ocean. The appearance of any given wave in one location is the overall expression of wavelets coming from all over the ocean. The movement of the boat at any moment is an expression of the total motion of the ocean as it folds into that particular region. Again, *we are an expression of the whole!*

To make this concept concrete, let's discuss the conception of a baby. A baby's life originates and takes form one fiery night when the grip of Eros overtakes her parents resulting in a wild and intimate display of affection. This loving embrace causes the baby to come into being. However, in life, as it is in dreams, things are not always the way they seem. There are other forces working alongside the blazing arrows of Eros in a baby's conception. Her mother's reproductive cycle has to be at the right phase for the baby to come into being. On the average, that cycle is 28 days and corresponds to the cycles of the moon. The moon has her part to play in the baby's conception. Similarly, the Earth affects the moon in her orbit around her as the moon affects the Earth in her orbit around the sun. In so affecting the moon, all these dancing celestial bodies define the mother's menstrual cycle. Each has a hand to play in baby's creation. We should pay homage to all these in celebrating the new life.

We could go on and on with this, forever and ever. We could examine the mood of the baby's father, not to mention the viability of his sperm, on that glorious night she becomes. We could relate that mood to the moon, the weather, farm or stock market prices, his biological clock in relationship to the cosmos and his fantasies throughout the day. As we would continue in our examination of that fruitful night of the baby's conception, we eventually would come to realize the entire universe took part in her creation. Extrapolating from this insight, we could conclude everything causes everything else. We come to the butterfly in China affecting the weather in New York phenomenon.

As we all know, children often look like their parents and take on their behavioral characteristics. We may describe the baby as having her father's eyes or her mother's nose. Or, we may say she "acts just like her father." All of these attributes arrange themselves in a creative fashion and are parts of the unique makeup that is the baby's form and personality. From a holistic perspective, this translates into the notion that everything mirrors everything else. As a woman, the baby girl mirrors the feminine function of the unmanifest. She is just like her Mother. As the unmanifest enfolds and unfolds the manifest, the baby enfolds the eggs that unfold and take form as her children through the impulse of her future lover. She enfolds these eggs within her body, as the soils of the Earth enfolds the seeds that blossom as flowers and trees at the loving kiss of the sun's rays. She enfolds these eggs in her womb as we enfold the insights in the fount of our minds that unfold upon hearing the fertilizing words of another human being. When the baby becomes a woman and one of her eggs begins to form, her womb contains the fetus in an amniotic fluid identical in content to seawater. The baby's womb mirrors the oceans of the Earth and the oceans of the Earth mirror the primal ocean of energy as the unmanifest. All creatures praise God in their being.

In our concrete example of the baby, we used objects that appear to us as solid, such as the moon, the Earth and the sun. However, according to the Hamilton-Jacobs theory, everything results from the actions of waves dancing upon an ocean of energy. The question is: how do we get from dancing waves to solid objects, such as moons, planets and suns? As an answer, Meister Eckhart asks, "Does the Soul wish to know the nature of a horse, a man, a woman, a planet? She creates an image!" (Underhill, 1990, p. 6) Similarly, chaos theorist Brian Steensma (2006) states:

Every thought, every sound, everything, if we can imagine, has transformed itself infinitely many times through the manifestations of every other thing across all frequencies and between all dimensions. Thus, a thing's natural state, from the viewpoint of infinity is absolute nothingness. From our perspective, presently, everything manifests according to our interpretation and perception. Any sound can be manifested as any other once you fly through the heart of infinite possibility. Everything is an expression of Krsna (sic). All memory is His memory. In the most specific sense, reality is an individual creation. In the broadest sense, reality is a consensus creation collectively perceived by all beings. The shape of the universe sounds like whatever the Infinite Being is thinking Right NOW. Everything is infinite dimensional Love right NOW for all eternity.

Neurologist Karl Pribram (Talbot, 1991) has been instrumental in understanding the brain from this holographic viewpoint. Simultaneous to the work of Bohm and other physicists, Pribram developed a holographic model of the brain based on findings that specific memories were *not* location specific in the brain. These findings contradicted the major tenets of other research into the brain's functioning.

Before Pribram and his colleagues, research into the brain assumed the memory trace of an event could be located in a specific spot in the brain. For example, the famous neurosurgeon, Wilder Penfield, would stimulate specific sites in the brain during an operation and elicit specific memories. This research, with epileptic patients, suggested memory was location specific. However, conclusions from these experiments have not held fast. The results only applied to epileptic patients. In surgeries requiring removal of a section of the brain associated with a particular memory with patients diagnosed with non-epileptic disorders, the patient did not have a gap in memory. Their memory was still intact. This type of result is incongruent with memory being location specific.

Neurophysiologist Karl Lashley, Pribram's former mentor, replicated these findings in his laboratory. In testing the location of memory, Lashley would train rats to run a maze. Upon the rats' mastery of the task, he would remove sections of their brains. To his surprise, he found no matter how much brain tissue he removed; the rats could still run the maze. Findings such as these blatantly contradicted the notion that memory was location specific.

Pribram's theories flourished further upon reading an article on holography in a mid 1960's edition of *Scientific American.* Lashley's findings combined with his own and his new understanding of holography led Pribram to further theorize that there was a distribution of specific memories throughout the brain that was similar to the distribution of the apple's image on the holographic plate described earlier. Indeed, he began to theorize the brain worked in a fashion similar to a holograph. Interestingly, at the time of this development, Pribram did not have access to the work of Bohm, who was theorizing the entire cosmos was a hologram. It was not until the 1970's that Pribram learned of Bohm through his son, who was a physicist. This is another example of synchronicity. As Steensma's quotation from above reveals, Sophia's web connects disparate minds to the Wisdom of the universal Mind. Again we see how each part mirrors the whole holographically. Pribram and Bohm were scientific surfers riding the same wave.

As discussed, physicists using the holistic model theorized nothing is solid. Perceived reality is a conglomerate of waves dancing upon an infinite ocean of energy. The puzzle is: How in the world does a person come to see anything as solid? When we touch a person or look upon a rock, we feel and see these manifestations as solid. We do not see a conglomeration of waves. Using the holographic model, Pribram theorized that, upon the perception of a wave, our brains mathematically construct objective reality. We do this by interpreting frequencies that are ultimately projections from another dimension, a deeper order of existence beyond time and space.

Objective reality does not exist in the way we believe it to exist. What is "out there" is a vast ocean of waves and frequencies. A newborn baby does not see a chair, a face, a dress, or a flower. He sees a vast and chaotic panorama of flowing colors and shapes, which his neocortex, once trained, will learn to differentiate and name according to the "norms" of his culture. Reality only looks concrete because our brain (a wave and frequency itself) has an ability to take these frequencies and convert them into images. In knowing this, one can almost hear Meister Eckhart laugh as he asks, "Does the Soul wish to know a horse, a car, a man? – She creates an image!" Science has rediscovered what ancients knew all along. Call it progress if you wish.

FOURIER TRANSFORMS

The way the Soul appears to do this magic is through a type of calculus, known as *Fourier Transforms*. These transforms were discovered by a man named Jean Fourier, who developed complex formulas to convert any pattern, no matter how complex, into the language of simple waves. He further used these formulas to transform the waves back into the original pattern. These formulas enabled a man named Gabor to develop holography. They further enabled him to convert objects into patterns of waves and back again into a three-dimensional image.

At first glance, it would appear calculus and brain function would have nothing to do with one another. However, in the late 60s and early 70s, various researchers contacted Pribram and told him they had uncovered evidence that our visual system worked as a type of frequency analyzer. How this happens was in question. The researchers realized our visual system was analyzing frequencies of waves. However, the mechanics of this analysis baffled them. The bright light of insight finally shone on this puzzle in 1979, when Berkeley neurophysiologists, Karen and Russell DeValois, discovered that the brain was using Fourier Transforms to convert waves into visual images!

Think on this for a moment. First, when you gaze into your lover's eyes or snuggle with your child before putting her to bed, you are gazing upon or cuddling with a waveform. You are a wave embracing a wave. According to current theory in physics, the transubstantiation of wave into particle, allowing you the sensation of solidity, is brought about by your attentiveness to your beloved. This means you and your child jointly create what you see and touch. Second, Fourier's brain "knew" and used the math long before he explicated his mathematical theory. His brain was using the mathematics he developed all along, unbeknownst to his conscious, academic mind. This means that in our depths, in the integral wholeness of our being that merges body/mind/spirit, we are in full knowledge. In ignorance, we call it progress when our conscious mind rediscovers what our bodies and subconscious minds have always known. This reveals why the Greek definition of *education* is *to bring forth*. Education is a revelation of what we already know. The knowledge is in the student; the teacher is a catalyst for its unfolding! Third, the process of Fourier's discovery serves as an example of Bohm's unmanifest implicate order. Jean Fourier enfolded the knowledge of Fourier Transforms within himself and unfolded that knowledge once he was ready for them to unfold! Just think of what lies within all of us as potential awaiting birth!

When my wife, Merry, was giving birth to her daughter, her obstetrician told her a "joke," illustrating how our bodies know more than our conscious mind can comprehend:

> *Can you scoop up sand and water in your hands and let the sand run out while retaining the water? No? I don't see why not. Any old asshole can do it!*

The taste and timing of his joke may have been questionable, but the wisdom underlying it is marvelous.

Further research into brain functioning has revealed that all our perceptions occur through an analysis of frequencies. When we view a person, make love, have a baby, hear a thought, taste a piece of candy or sit on a couch, we are interpreting frequencies of waves. For fifty years I only "saw" two types of trees: deciduous and evergreen. Only as I turned my attention to my responsibility to heal the ecological damage to the little bit of Earth on my "property," did the beautiful variations of birch, ash, maple, pine, fir, and spruce become real for me. Now the tamarack, which drops its needles seasonally, and the holly, which does not drop its leaves, blur the categories I once thought I "knew." A thought is a wave. It is vibrating energy. It is a Word arising from its ground as we attend to it and dissolving back into its ground as our attention wanders.

In the next chapter, we will have some fun discussing sexuality as a holographic expression of universal process. Just as Fourier enfolded his calculus within himself, our sexuality will be found as enfolding the secrets to the cosmos. "Nature and Mind are a necessary unity," Bateson (1985) says. Nature generates us in her image and we hold all her secrets within ourselves. How could it be otherwise?

Chapter 7
Cosmic Sex

Gender is everything:
Everything has its Masculine and Feminine Principles;
Gender manifests on all planes.
~ The Three Initiates (1912, p. 183)

*I*ce-dancers weave gracefully towards and away from each other. Separated, they reach their arms towards each other, longing to feel each other's embrace. Together, the male takes his bride and lifts her into the height of joyful ecstasy. Viewers thrill to this metaphor for the universal dance between male and female. In Greek mythology it lives as the dance of Psyche (the human Soul) and Eros (divine Love). It lives in each of us in the strands of our DNA, which weave apart and together repeatedly in the perpetual dance of creative Love. Generation after generation, we retell this primal story in our love lives. The ice dance is the dance of all life. It is the dance of God with creation. All creation dances the steps of division or separation from the divine Creativity and then of joyful reunion.

Interestingly, we often call intercourse, the union of female with male, "sex." However, in its etymology, "sex" means to divide and is related to such words as "dissect." It reflects the differentiation and division of male and female. It also reflects the processes of conception and birth, which, again, are processes of division or separation.

After the glorious union of sperm with egg that meld to form a single cell, that cell immediately divides, forming first two, then multiple cells that become increasingly differentiated yet remain one fetus. Again we see the cosmic dance of distinction and unity. This dance reaches its climax in birth, the ultimate process of separation of child from mother. They are drawn together again, as the baby suckles, in the intimate exchange of nursing, only to separate at weaning and, increasingly, throughout childhood, culminating in the rebellious years of adolescence. Yet, it is at this time of ultimate separation that the grown child seeks out his Beloved and unites once more in glorious sexual union, beginning the process all over again. ...And the dance goes on!

MARRYING ATHENA

As a child in middle school, I was introduced to Greek myth and was, for the most part, bored with what I heard–that was, until I heard of Athena, the Goddess of Wisdom. My ears perked up in learning about her, while my body sparkled in an invisible fiery display of love. I was never more alive than at that moment. The grips of Eros caused me to lose all sense of myself as I vowed to marry her. Yet, I realized I had to keep my passions secret. How was I going to break the news to my mother that I was destined to marry a Goddess living on Mount Olympus? Yet, as the creation of this book reveals, I have been true to those vows, though I have been unconscious of them during a large portion of my life.

In hearing of Athena, I fully understood intuitively why she was a woman or Goddess. As Wisdom, She conceived thought. This was common sense to me. I basically was linking the feminine to the process of conception. My thinking was based on an inchoate assumption that I would conceptualize consciously only much later: *gender is an active process or function, more than it is a passive state-of-being.* Gender is a verb more so than a noun.

It occurred to me at that time that conception of a thought happens very much like conception of a baby. Both are internal processes. While I could not have verbalized my insight in such a mature way, I fundamentally understood that when I absorb the thoughts of another, their thoughts function as seminal influences for conception within myself. Their thoughts fulfill the masculine role of enlivening the hitherto latent seed of thought within me. I must then gestate this new thought and bring it forth into the shared world. To my eyes, this process of sexual creation appeared to manifest in many forms throughout the universe. I saw the same process at work in Mother Earth's absorption of the sun's rays and the subsequent unfolding of flowers in the spring.

As an adult, I found my ideas about gender supported by various spiritual teachings throughout the world. The Taoists have long taught, for instance, that we are all a marriage of the receptive, gestating female principle, *yin,* and the active, fertilizing male principle, *yang.* I did not, however, find such an open regard for sexuality within my own society or within Christianity, *as it was culturally transmitted to me.* In this chapter, I would like to expose how the Bible does, in fact, express these ideas then relate Biblical teachings to spiritual teachings from other traditions regarding our sexual nature. In this way, we can understand our maleness and femaleness as being spiritually exhibited throughout the universe and know ourselves, male and female, as mirrors of the God of creation.

HUMAN AND DIVINE CONCEPTION

Upon an egg's absorption of sperm, she begins to divide into a variety of cells and ultimately becomes a human being. This process mirrors creation myths from throughout the world. For example, consider the following lines from the Bible's Book of Genesis:

> *And the Earth was without form and void; and darkness was upon the face of the Deep. And the Spirit moved out over the face of the Waters.*
>
> *And God said, 'Let there be Light'; and there was Light.*
>
> *And God saw the Light, that it was good; and God divided the Light from the Darkness and God called the light Day and the darkness He called Night. And the Evening and the Morning were the first day.*
>
> *And God said, "Let there be a firmament in the midst of the Waters and let it divide the Waters from the Waters."*

To understand how Genesis mirrors human conception, we need to understand the gender of nouns in the original Hebrew language used. Just about the entire opening verse uses nouns in the feminine gender. The Earth, the Deep and the Waters all refer to the feminine Tehom (Baring and Cashford, 1991). Since Marie means ocean, we could also refer to Tehom as Marie. The spirit that moved over the Waters of Genesis moved over Mary in the virgin birth story in the New Testament. This spirit, as we have mentioned, became identified as Sophia.

The virgin birth of Jesus in the New Testament is analogous to the virgin birth of humanity in the Old Testament. Hence, John 1:14 says, "And the Word was made flesh." The Word is the commandment, "Let there be...," arising from the depths of Tehom that created this world. What God thinks becomes! No wonder some physicists are now saying that the universe behaves more like a thought than a machine. Again, the Word, constituted of vibratory waves containing information, *IS* made flesh. Those waves are absorbed by the eyes and lead to the creation of an image inside our minds. At every instant in time we recreate that which God created in eternity. Truly, he shares himself with us in this creative process. In this context, our sexuality and every other aspect of our being can be seen as holy.

In the light of these insights, the duel between proponents of intelligent design and the proponents of evolution rooted in sexuality becomes moot. This is not an either/or question, but rather a question to which the answer is a resounding "Yes!" All that we see, hear, and touch in the world is both evolved and designed by intelligence–both the infinite/eternal Intelligence of Wisdom and the here/now intelligence of each observer.

The term originally used in Genesis for Spirit was the feminine Ruach. Many identified this Ruach as Sophia, the Spirit of Wisdom and Understanding, whose symbol was the dove. The dove continues appearing to this day as a symbol for the Christian Holy Spirit (Baring and Cashford, 1991). This Spirit was said to move upon the face of the Waters. The dove moving, brooding, arising or dancing upon the water was a common symbol for the Goddess in ancient times, including: Aphrodite, Inanna, Ishtar, Isis and Eurynome. For example, Eurynome (Universal One) danced upon the Primordial Ocean in bringing the primordial elements to order. She then created a Great Serpent who served as her male lover.

The idea of the world being void and without form also means the world exists in the beginning as a potential waiting to unfold. This is why the number "0" is egg shaped, in the same shape as the opening to a woman's vulva. "0" is the universe in potential. This accounts for unborn thoughts within you as well as accounting for the universe's existence prior to the Big Bang. It is natural law. In the beginning, emptiness contains the Word in his formless state, just as a pregnant pause contains unspoken words yet to form and be given expression. Is the cup half empty or half full? The answer is yes. What is empty defines what is full in the eternally unified dance of yin and yang.

The second verse in the Bible then leads to the arising of the Word. "And God said." Just as the egg divides upon absorbing the sperm, it is the Word that causes the Primordial Waters to divide, diversify, and ultimately become the created universe. From our human perspective, it is upon the absorption of light or sound waves containing information that we create an image or hear and interpret a sound. Hence, the feminine no-thing conceives some-thing from her substance in relation to the male some-thing. If it were not for the male act of dividing through presentation of information, there would be no distinctions and hence we could not "know" anything. Duality is a necessary condition for self-knowledge. Duality is as essential to an appreciation of unity as darkness is to an appreciation of light.

This masculine act of division and diversification is reflected in the phallic number "1." It is at the point "1" arises that division begins to occur, which in Genesis is reflected in the division of light from dark. One arises from zero and hence there are two, "0" (the shape of the egg or vulva) and "1." The existence of these "2" automatically generates "3," which is the love child of no-thing and some-thing, dark and light or female and male. Hence the letter for Alpha in the Roman alphabet, "A", is composed of two lines emerging from a single point, separating, yet bridged by a third line linking the two together. Love is the power that bridges everything. Eros leads us to wholeness.

This creative, formative process mirrors human conception at the point when the sperm dissolves into the egg and initiates a process of division, diversification, and formation within the egg. The very first act of the fertilized egg is to divide in two, just as light and dark divide in the beginning of Genesis.

The modern mathematician, G. Spencer-Brown (1972), addresses this process when he claims that the first order of the universe is "Let there be distinction."

Interested to see just how widespread this transactive--not to mention erotic–concept of the creative process might be, I began to look closely at the creation myths of many different cultures. In the process, I also discovered a metaphorical link to the process of eating. To understand the creation stories and their relationship to sexual reproduction and eating, I often meditate on the image of the Egyptian Goddess, Nut, swallowing and giving birth to the Sun God, Ra.

The image expresses the overall process of how the universe works. It is more than a metaphoric image of the sun rising in the morning and setting in the evening. It speaks to the function of the heart as it recreates the energy level of blood, as well as the land as it becomes dormant in the wintertime and brings forth life in the spring. The Nut and Ra image is also reflective of sexuality, for the male springs from the womb and returns to the womb of a woman in sex and to the womb of Mother Earth in death. In both returns he serves to generate new life. Whenever we eat, we kill and consume life in order to sustain and regenerate life in a new form. In sex, this process is seen in the sperm eagerly seeking the enticing egg, dissolving within her, surrendering his form and energy to join with hers, completing the cycle of life and death so rebirth can commence in the formation of a unique, new human being.

A corresponding process of sexual reproduction takes place for plants as well as animals, forever creating unique new holographs of the universe. This shows that every living being must eat and be eaten in order to be reborn. Sex is about recreation and occurs universally. The process is the way and the way is reflected in sexuality that is another form of eating. Yes, there is a relation between a bright red tomato enticing your mouth to water to fulfill its desire to have its seeds spread about with an image of a plump and erect penis wanting to find a home for its seeds inside a moist vagina.

Sex reveals how the universe works in bringing forth potential from within. In the consummate joining of yin with yang, the creation of the universe is reenacted, producing a unique new being. Hence, God is said to create humanity in His image, "male and female created He them" (Genesis 1:27). Sex is universal and not separate from God. God caused the genders to divide and sexuality to evolve, because he loves both the female and the male within his self! The love between woman and man is the love God has for herself, which is then made manifest in human form. We look at sexual union in another way when we come to see that our desire for each other manifests as a means to reclaim our wholeness. We never feel as complete and validated as after lovemaking (unless our copulation is devoid of Love, in which case we never feel as isolated and shameful). As the Tantric practitioners realize, sex is a quest for the ecstasy of unity with the Divine. Yes, it is possible to invite God into the most intimate aspects of your being!

God contains both the male and the female principles. The primary functions of his femininity are to give birth, sustain, integrate or marry, receive or dissolve, and devour and absorb. The functions of her masculinity are to penetrate, impregnate and initiate the diversification that leads to new life. What is unified becomes many through the powers of the male; what is separate becomes one through the powers of the female. Perhaps this is the reason why one of the original names for God in Hebrew is Elohim, comprising the singular feminine, *Eloh,* and the plural masculine, *im.*

For example, everyone reading this book began as an egg nestled in the ovaries of a woman and a sperm dancing in the testicles of a man. For every menstrual cycle, usually one egg is released from the ovaries. During the span of our mother's entire life, even during the time of our formation in her uterus, we existed within our mother's body as a possibility waiting to unfold. In our mother's adulthood, the egg destined to become us emerged from the ovaries during a period of ovulation. A sperm generated amongst millions of other sperms from our father's testicles sought out and penetrated the egg during this ripe and fertile time and dissolved within it. Our mother's egg then absorbed the genetic messages contained in the sperm, married them with her own, and began to divide exponentially into a variety of cells. Ultimately, the egg became us. Moreover, it hasn't stopped its journey upon emerging from the womb of our human mother. It continues to unfold its potential within the nurturing body of Mother Earth including her breath, the atmosphere. It continues to draw energy given to the Earth by the fathering Sun. The nurturing embrace of the Earth is but another womb on a larger scale in which we unfold our potentials.

CHILDREN OF MOTHER NATURE

We are the children of Mother Nature, bearing the stamp of her genetics, as truly as we are the children of our human mothers and fathers. As such, our spinal columns could be seen as mirroring trees and our bloodstream as river systems with all their tributaries. The firing of neurons in our brains could be seen as mirroring the stars glittering in deep space or the dance of lightning in the air. Our vaginas appear, in this metaphorical thinking, as deep caves leading to the riches hidden in darkness; while our penises appear as explorers of the deep or as delightful fruits reaching forth to entice creation, much as an apple entices us, with its redness and aroma, to eat so its seed could be spread about. In this regard, Nature contains both yin and yang, as do we. Nature is as much our Father as our Mother, for God and Nature are one.

Furthermore, Nature, meaning Essence, is reflected in our labors, or what we produce from within ourselves. What we produce in our art or our work reflects us, just as any child reflects its parents and ancestors. This is independent of whether we take the form of a man or a woman. Again, the Inner Feminine that labors in all creative acts is the essence of our being and all acts of creation reflect their Mother-Source.

The Judeo-Christian Bible tells us:

Remember, Oh man, that thou art dust;
Dust thou art and to dust returnest.

This Biblical injunction does not have to be read as negatively as it often is. Yes, it puts us "in our place," squarely as the offspring of Mother Earth. Soil is the womb of the Mother, teeming with life, more extensive than the life we view above the planetary surface, and providing the sustenance for new life. The energy of our spirit and body is not lost. No energy is ever lost, just transformed. Within the soil–as, indeed, within our guts–beneficial bacteria thrive, acting in symbiotic relationship with our life energy to produce what we need to become to fulfill the great plan of our Creator.

GLOBAL CREATION STORIES
The Biblical story of creation is mirrored in creation myths throughout the world and transcends religious boundaries. For example, mirroring the account in Genesis, in Orphic Greek mythology the first distinction arose after Lord Eros erupted from the egg laid by the Goddess Nyx, meaning Uncreated Night. His eruption caused the egg to split into Heaven and Earth just as the human egg divides in half upon fertilization or as the Word divides Tehom into night and day.

In medieval Europe, the Christian Mystic, Jacob Boehme wrote this version of creation:

> *For the Nothing causeth the Willing, that it is Desirous; and the Desiring is an Imagination...Wherein the Will, in the Looking-Glass of Wisdome, discovereth It Selfe...and impregnateth It Selfe with the Imagination out of the Wisdome, viz: out of the Virgin-like Looking Glass, which there is a Mother...For, the Will, viz: the Father, speaketh...in the Looking-Glass of Wisdome...and openeth the Word of Life.*(Schipflinger, 1998, p. 198)

In Boehme's creation story, the primordial Waters (Nothing) give birth to the Willing. Interestingly, the Greek, Hermes, says that Wisdom is our womb of birth and Will is our begetter. Will is simultaneously a desire and a command. It reflects the unity of Eros and Logos or Desire and Word. Hence, God wills light or the manifest to be born of the dark unmanifest or nothing by his spoken Word, "Let there be...."

The Rig Veda (10.129) recounts the Indian Hindu creation story this way:

> *There was neither death nor immortality then. There was no distinguishing sign of night or day. That one breathed,*

windless, by its own impulse. Other than that there was nothing beyond.

Darkness was hidden by darkness in the beginning; with no distinguishing sign, all this was Water. The Life Force that was covered with Emptiness, that one arose through the power of heat.

Desire came upon that one in the beginning; that was the first seed of mind. Poets seeking in their heart with Wisdom found the bond of existence in non-existence. (Doniger, 1981, p. 25)

Later in the *Rig Veda*: 10.125 (p. 63), the Life Force that was covered in emptiness speaks:

I am the Queen, the confluence of riches, the skillful one who is first among those worthy of sacrifice. The Gods divided me up into various parts, for I dwell in many places and enter into many forms.

The one who eats food, who truly sees, who breathes, who hears what is said, does so through me. Though they do not realize it, they dwell in me. Listen, you whom they have heard: What I tell you should be heeded.

I am the one who says, by myself, what gives joy to gods and men. Whom I love I make awesome; I make him a sage, a wise man, a Brahmin.

I stretch forth the bow for Rudra so that his arrow will strike down the hater of prayer. I incite the contest among the people. I have pervaded sky and Earth.

I give birth to the Father on the head of this world. My womb is in the Waters, within the Ocean. From there, I spread out over all creatures and touch the very sky with the crown of my head.

I am the one who blows like the wind, embracing all creatures. Beyond the sky, beyond this Earth, so much have I become in my greatness.

This blowing like the wind is obviously related to the Spirit that moved across the face of the Waters in Genesis, which is again repeated in the virgin birth story of our Lord Jesus who is born of the Virgin Mary or Ocean (i.e., Marie or Marine). In reading this passage, our western sensibilities may become distraught with the idea of sacrifice. However, the term *sacrifice* simply means *to make whole.* If you ever "die" to yourself and experience your wholeness, you will understand these words.

The Siviate Sutra, also a Hindu text from India, shines further light upon the role of the Word, a vibration, in creation:

> *The Initiating Point desirous to manifest the Thought it holds of all things, vibrates, transformed into the primordial sound of the nature of a cry. It shouts out the universe, which is not distinct from Itself. That is to say; It thinks it. Hence, the term Word. Meditation is the supreme Word. It Sounds, that is to say, vibrates, submitting all to the fragmentation of Life. This is how it is vibration. This is what is meant by the saying: 'Sound, which is of the nature of a cry, resides in all things.* (Danielou, Alain, 1943, p. 7)

Note the similarities in the Keres Pueblo Native American story of creation:

> *Ooma-oo, long ago. The Spider (Thinking Woman) was in the place where only she was. There was no light or dark; there was no warm wind, no rain or thunder. There was no cold, no ice or snow. There was only the Spider. She was a great Wise Woman, whose powers are beyond imagining. No medicine person, no conjurer or shaman, no witch or sorcerer, no scientist or inventor can imagine how great her power is. Her power is complete and total. It is pure and clear. It is the power of thought, we*

say, but not the kind of thought people do all the time. It's like the power of dream, but more pure. Like the spirit of vision, but more clear. It has no shape or movement because it just is. It is the power that creates all that is and it is the power of all that is....

...She was so happy with what she knew, so full of awe at the beauty of the Song, that she thought again. And again she knew the rippling, the wrinkling, the running of spidery lines along the edges of the forming pouch of the power's Song, the folding and enfolding into a shape that held some of the power of all that is within. She knew that the place of that pouch, that bundle of her thought, her Song, was in the Northeast. So humming and Singing, she shaped them. Humming and singing, she placed them where they belonged. That was how the directions came into being. How the seasons came to be.

She thought in her power to each of the bundles and continued singing. She sang and sang. She sang the power that was her heart, the movement that is the universe and its dancing. The power that is everywhere and that has no name or body, but that is just the power, the mystery. She sang and the bundles began to move. They began to sing, to echo (mirror) her Song, to join it. They sang their heart's song that was the same as Spider's heart Song that was the heart Song of the Great Mystery, the power that moves...

(Allen, 1991, p. 34–35)

Notably similar themes again emerge in the Middle Eastern *Stanzas of Dyzan:*

The last vibration of the seventh Eternity thrills through Infinitude. The Mother swells, expanding from within without, like the bud of a lotus.

The vibration sweeps along, touching with its swift wing the entire universe and the germ that dwelleth in Darkness: the Darkness that breathes over the slumbering Waters of Life.

Darkness radiates Light and Light drops one solitary ray into the Mother's Depths. The ray shoots through the virgin egg, the ray causes the eternal egg to thrill and drop the non-eternal germ, which condenses into the world egg.

Then, the three fall into four. The radiant Essence becomes seven inside, seven outside, the luminous egg which in itself is three, curdles and spreads in milk white curds throughout the Depths of Mother, the root that grows in the Depths of the Primordial Ocean of Life.

The root remains, the Light remains, the curds remain; still Oeahoo is One. (Iyer, 1988, p. 84)

Such accounts of creation are meditations on the conception of the universe through the arising of the Word. Basic to these meditations is the idea that the Word, sometimes called Thought, Sound or Desire are the powers that generate division within the Virgin. The meditations are from different areas of the world and reflect different religions, yet we can see a holographic pattern emerging.

The myths of sexual creation from so many cultures are so similar that we can draw from them a single universal story: In the beginning there was darkness. There was no movement, no sound. There were no people, no animals. There was nothing at all, not even time or space. Indeed, in this state, a moment and an eternity are one and the same, for this is Infinity and Infinity is without boundaries. Then, suddenly, this purity was broken by the impulse of Love desiring a focus for its passion. This Love inseminated the dark void, the Mother, in order to form all things. In this sense, we finite beings truly are a light in our Mother's eye. We memorialize this conception every time we have a great idea and call it *brilliant* or say, "A light just went on in my head." In these statements, we are seeing into our kinship with the universal Mother, for we are her bright idea. We are all light-beings.

The only difference between the universal story manifested in diverse creation myths and human conception is that the Word or Desire is both born of the Primordial Waters and initiates her diversification into all living things. He is both a son and a lover. Unless there is a deep pathology, a man does not function as son and lover to the same woman. Yet, he does function in both these capacities to womankind. Every individual woman ultimately transcends herself and opens into an expression of the Goddess. Man as son is born of woman, usually headfirst. As a lover, he returns to her, headfirst. This is why ancient Greeks realized the Goddess as mother and fate; beginning and end; birth and death; alpha and omega. How many a man has entered ecstasy in surrendering to his beloved! Of course, men fear this loss of self and reflect this fear in the avoidance of intimacy about which women often complain. Fear of women, fear of death, fear of feelings, and fear of the sea are all related, as we shall explore in the next chapter.

Chapter 8
The Ocean of Life

She is the innermost awareness of the sage who
realizes that Consciousness alone exists.
She is the life blossoming within the creatures of the
universe. Both macrocosm and microcosm
are lost in the Mother's womb......When anyone
attempts to know Her, the singer of this song laughs.
Can you swim across a shoreless ocean?
Yet, the child in me still reaches out to touch the moon.
–Ramprasad (Hixon, 1994, p.44)

Beyond this world of time and space, Mother Sophia stands alone, complete unto herself. Sophia is not anything or anybody. Indeed, she has no characteristics at all. She just is. That is, she is all. Or, she is not! Sophia is unconditioned existence, pure being and the Nature of all that is. She is Ramprasad's *shoreless ocean*. Her dance is a striptease for she reveals herself as Truth, the naked essence of all that lives. She is our "*isness*," our Divine Isis, the Roman version of the Egyptian *Au-Set* or *Throne of Power*. Sophia is our beloved Virgin Mother whose beauty is incomprehensible to human imagination. After all, who is there in this vast universe that can describe or comprehend infinite Wisdom? Any attempts at conceptualizing Sophia will fail, for she is an unfathomable Ocean of Life with no shores, whose depths are without beginning or end. She is an ineffable and unthinkable silence beyond sense, perception or thought. Formless and void, Sophia is the great abyss who exists as a dazzling and translucent darkness outshining all the suns in the visible skies. All these surface structures are mere shadows of her infinite light, her timeless consciousness.

In the beginning, Sophia envelops everything in a formless state. Through an impulse of Love, she envisions the form of all creatures. Her dream swirls within her. In her womb, she creates swirling galaxies, dancing planets, flying birds, prancing animals and thought-provoking people. All these creatures express Sophia and Sophia expresses all these creatures. In awe of the beauty of her dream, Sophia becomes desirous to give expression to the infinite variety of creatures and characteristics she holds within. The dream arising from her depths sings. He is a beautiful harmony whispering in her ears. The dream is her baby and she calls him "Light". The wine of joy intoxicates Sophia. In ecstasy, she "hums" the Song of Creation to her dream children. By her voice, she forms them. With a tender kiss, she seduces them into awakening as the universal dance.

Sophia's Song is radiant and beautiful. He is the passionate light of her dream and he dances naked before the Mother. Sophia loves, worships, and adores him. Her entire body vibrates with the beautiful harmony of her son and the unborn beings she contains within begin to form. She dances wildly and swirls about in ecstasy. Her womb thrills; her body swells; she cries out in the pain of joy. Her entire body shakes at intensities beyond the experiences and fantasies of the human mind. Finally, with one massive thrust, Sophia's children burst from between her thighs like water exploding from a ruptured dam. Swirling galaxies, spinning planets, explosive stars, beautiful plants, powerful animals and curious people begin to form as they erupt from the Mother.

The entire universe dances and swims in joy. It is alive. It is majestic. It is the expression of the unfathomable Sophia. Everything forms in worship of her, in accordance to her command. Human women form in imitation of their Mother. Men form in imitation of Her Son. Women fold inward to find her within; men fold outward to seek her manifestation. It is all a beautiful dance. Everything fits; everything works perfectly; everything dances in unison. Every creature is a symphony arising, growing and dissolving within the oceanic presence of our Beloved Sophia, the Inner Nature of all that is. Nothing dies; nothing ceases to exist. There is only a return to Sophia.

Sophia's children love her and call her by various names. No matter what names they call her, She is their Mother, their source of life, and their eternal resting home. Women and men who remember Sophia do not fear death. Men such as the Goddess intoxicated Hindu poet, Ramprasad, gaze death in the eye and sing praises to her:

> *The singer of this liberating song*
> *laughs loud and long:*
> *We shall be in the end*
> *what we were in the beginning,*
> *clear bubbles forming and dissolving*
> *in the stream of timeless Mother Wisdom."*
> (Hixon, 1994, p. 105)

We are clear bubbles arising and dissolving in an Ocean of Wisdom. How beautiful is the dance! Yet, we engage in spiritual debates on how our particular ideas about God are the correct ideas. In egocentricity we try to make others believe our ideas about God will save them from some type of hellish condition; either during manifestation on this Earth or in the afterlife. In our self-centered perceptions of God, our paying *witness* to the Divine Nature entails our becoming God's theological salespersons, instead of having a direct experience of our unity in God. May our ideas about God die so we can directly taste Her!

Within the field of spiritual thought, there is a debate about whether God is personal or impersonal. Christians generally espouse the view of the personal God and focus on their relationship with him. In contrast, many intellectual mystics who study God as a principle hold an impersonal God as supreme. I devote little energy to this debate. What would I know about these issues? I am but a child swimming playfully in the amniotic depths of Sophia.

Everywhere I look, I see her. I see her in the images arising, dancing and returning to the font of my mind and in the imagined form of my body. I further realize her as my body's ability to heal and to die. I know her as the life-supporting manure nourishing flowers in their growth, as well as in the flowers that grow and the agent behind their growth and dissolution. I know her in the Worm that nourishes them from below as well as the Sun that nourishes them from above. I further realize her as defining the relationship of flowers to the ecosystems at large. I then experience her in the microscopic atomic world, as well as in the incomprehensible number of stars in the nighttime sky. Everything existing within or without has its ground in my beloved Mother. She smiles at our notions of personal and impersonal God and disintegrates them into dust. When the dust clears, only Sophia remains. She alone is real for her essence is reflected in all her creations.

I often consider my search for Sophia as being similar to Dr. Livingstone's search for the source of the Nile. In my expedition, I am in search for my source; identified as an infinite ocean of consciousness from whom I arise. Livingstone's expedition is, perhaps, a metaphor for a similar search. Our individual Souls are like rivers flowing home to Sophia. They emerge from and return to her, just as the waters of any river originate in the ocean to evaporate into the air, rain upon the Earth, trickle into the rivers and eventually return to the sea to be cycled anew. There is no such thing as death. There is only a merging, a marriage of the two into one.

THE OCEAN METAPHOR IN VARIOUS CULTURES

The Ocean is a common symbol in both the human psyche and mythology. It refers to the depths of the psyche or Soul, our source of origin and our womb. Even if someone dreams of a turbulent ocean, she is dreaming of the source of her turbulence. This notion of the sea being our source relates to evolutionary biologists' speculations that all life on this planet first evolved in the sea. Mirroring this origin in the sea, the amniotic fluid that we breathed as a fetus was of the same content as seawater. A woman's uterus mirrors the Earth's uterus. The use of Holy Water in ancient spiritual rituals reflected this idea of a woman's body mirroring the Earth. Originally called "Mother's Elixir," Holy Water was of a high saline content that mirrored the content of amniotic fluid. Its application in ritual meant rebirth.

Not all manifest oceans are of water. We currently swim in an ocean of air we call the atmosphere. We breathe this air just as we breathed amniotic fluid in our mother's womb. In transcending the planet, we find planets, stars and galaxies floating in an ocean of space. This ocean mirrors the oceans of the Earth. It even has vibratory waves of light, sound and other pulsations dancing rhythmically through the so-called vacuum.

All of these things point towards our make-up. Our bodies are of the same content as seawater, while the composition of photons dancing throughout our bodies is more than 99.999% "empty space." We look just like our planetary Mother on the surface and our universal Mother in our depths.

Indeed, many scientists now theorize that there is no empty space. According to the government site, *Ask a Scientist*:

> *There is a baseline of energy everywhere in space, often described as 'soup' from which particles are constantly emerging and disappearing (maybe think of fishes diving out of water and landing back in). So there are not only the particles of the atom, but lots of other ones around too, all overlapping to some degree... The concept of 'space' is still very much a mystery.*

(www.newton.dep.anl.gov/askasci/phy05/phy05166.htm)

Ultimately, the oceans of water, air and space transcend themselves into the *"infinite ocean of energy"* that physicist David Bohm uses as a metaphor to explain the *Unmanifest Implicate Order* (Talbot, 1991). (See the discussion of Bohm's theory in chapter 6.) Bohm states the movements of this ocean are an enfolding and unfolding; thus he emphasizes the wholeness of the whole and the wholeness of the part. Significantly, a human embryo, at an early point in its evolution (unfolding) looks like a fish and even has what appear to be gills where his ears will eventually develop. At this stage, the fetus remembers the time in planetary evolution when he swam in the oceans of the Earth. Yet, the humanness of the fetus is already implicated or implied, awaiting manifestation. The evolution of the human fetus in the uterus is an unfolding of the humanity that existed in an implied state within him.

Bohm's theory mirrors that of the mystics. For example, 17th century Christian Mystic, Jacob Boehme, stated the

Primordial Abyss or Nothing is pure potential (Shipflinger, 1998, p. 198). Similarly, the Keres Pueblo, a Native American tribe, believed they lived in a cave alongside their Beloved Mother, Thinking Woman, alternatively called Spider Grandmother, before manifesting on this world. Mirroring the Keres, ancient Egyptians believed the Goddess Ma-Nu, enfolded all creatures in a formless state before manifesting them in this world. There is no point in which something does not exist. Before manifestation, everything exists in an implied state within the Mother. This idea manifests through the common Christian bumper sticker that says, "Long before you were formed in your mother's womb, God knew you."

The latter part of the Egyptian Goddess' name, Nu, serves as the foundation for another name of the sea Goddess: *Nun.* Interestingly, the Bible's Joshua was the son of Nun. His name is the Hebrew form of the Greek name, *Jesus.* Perhaps we can speculate he was born of the primordial ocean, Nun, just as Jesus was born of Marie. After all, Mary's name means ocean and is a cognate to Nun. Is this accidental coincidence, or is it Sophia's humor? You decide in your heart.

In the story, Joshua involved himself with a woman named Rehab. According to the Bible, she was a whore who aided his army in the conquest of Jericho. Whore in Hebrew is *hor,* meaning *hole, cavern, cave, or pit.* The term often served as a synonym for a sacred prostitute and the Goddess she served. Another Hebrew title for whore is *Zonah,* which also referred to a *prophetess.* One of the oldest Hebrew folk dances was the *hora,* named after an ancient circle dance of the sacred harlots. This dance unfolded from the Pagan *Dance of the Hours,* which began as an ancient European ceremony of the *Horae,* the *Divine Whores* who kept the hours of the night by dancing (Walkers, 1983, p. 821). The word *whore* evolved from the Persian *houri* and the Greek *horae,* which are terms forming the basis for our modern day *hour.*

In Egypt, it was common practice for the *Ladies of the Hour* to rule a certain hour of the night. It was their job to protect the solar boat of the Sun God Ra (also known as the Word) in His underworld (unmanifest) passage.

Perhaps the modern term *rehabilitation* unfolds from the name of the prostitute *Rehab*. To rehabilitate means *to restore to original condition*. This refers to our original condition of wholeness, for *Rehab* was originally a *prophetic Sea-Goddess and Guardian of Sheol*. Being a Sea-Goddess means she is Marie. Ancient Hebrews identified *Sheol* with the uninhabitable parts of the world (Graves, 1948, p. 476) and with paradise (Walker, 1983, p. 933). In Hebrew, *Sheol* means *Pit and* is a synonym for *hor*. Sheol relates to the uterine paradise-garden called *Shal-Mari* in Tibet and *Shalimar* in India. *Shalimar* is probably another name for the modern day paradise known as *Shambahla*. In its earliest form, Sheol was the Virgin's enclosed garden of flowers, fruits, fountains and fairy nymphs. Sacred Kings who died on trees went to this world of Sheol. This obviously relates to the death and resurrection of Christ into Heaven. It is a different manifestation of the same story.

The notion of a God born of a virgin who died and was resurrected was widespread in ancient times. The story of Lord Jesus is but one manifestation of a story that is universal. Sometimes the story emerged through ritual and allowed the worshipper of the Goddess to realize himself as a manifestation of the process. For example, within Orphic Greece, the ceremony of initiation into the mysteries entailed the devotee being swallowed by a great Sea-Dragon who served as a metaphor for the Mother. Upon his return to her belly, he transformed and was reborn as an incarnation of the Sun God (Matthews, 1994).

Could this mean that in letting go to what we think we are allows us to evolve? What is "letting go" if not a state of emptiness or a state beyond conditioning?

Another example of this process is the Celtic story of the transformation of little Gwion into the great poet Taliesin. According to the story, Taliesin's Mother, Cerdwin, was fixing a brew that would help her other son, an ugly duckling, become beautiful. However, Gwion saw the potion and swallowed it. Having drunk what was intended for his brother, Gwion infuriates his Mother. She soon gave chase to him at which point he would turn himself into various animals and she, in turn, would turn into that animal's predator. For example, if he became a rabbit, she would become a fox. Gwion finally turned himself into a seed and his Mother swallowed him in the form of a crow. After spending 9 months inside her, he was reborn as the poet, Taliesin.

ANCIENT AND MODERN CAVE RITUALS

This death-rebirth process was often symbolized through rituals in caves during ancient times. This is why Lord Jesus was said to have lain in a cave for three days before his resurrection. Throughout the world, from Native America to the Orient, the cave served as a metaphor for womb. In Europe, the initiate would enter the belly of the dark and mysterious cave, at which time he would receive the initiation rites and spiritual instruction of the Goddess. Upon reentering the world, the surrounding culture would know the initiate as a poet and lover of the Mother (Graves, 1948). These types of initiations helped one confront death and realize who one was...the eternal Son of the Goddess. It was a process of realization, self-discovery and heightened awareness.

The metaphor continues to this day in movies such as *Dead-Poets Society*. In this movie, a group of boys being schooled in a stifling educational environment find a cave and go into it to learn the art of poetry writing. Upon their first time in the cave, there is a haunting sound of an owl.

The owl was seen as the Bird of Athena (Wisdom) in ancient Greece and was oftentimes the bird of death. As we have discussed, death is the essence of rebirth.

The purpose of poetry writing, as the boys' rebellious teacher (played by Robin Williams) points out, is to "woo women," i.e., the Goddess. As such, the boys ultimately are reborn as poets and wind up confronting the school authorities. In other words, they transcended their current condition and entered a new life. Like Gwion, the boys in the movie were reborn after entering the body of the Mother and stood up to the powers that oppressed them. No wonder the Goddess is so dangerous! No wonder the extreme patriarchies manifested in fundamentalist sects, be they Christian or Muslim, abuse women to suppress them. Healthy, assertive women give birth to children that are healthy and assertive!

In the Bible, the Primordial Ocean of Genesis I:2 was divided and ultimately formed into creation. The same process also manifested in Babylon, through their creation myth known as the *Enuma Elish*. In that story, the Goddess was the Sea Serpent known as Great Ocean Mommu Tiamant. The Sun God or Word was Marduk. In *Genesis*, the division of the Waters by the Word is relatively peaceful. In the Babylonian account presented below, it is bloody and violent:

> *He heaped up a mountain over Tiamant's head,*
> *pierced her eyes to form the sources of the Tigris and*
> *Euphrates*
> *and heaped similar mountains over her dugs,*
> *which he pierced to make the rivers*
> *from the eastern mountains that flow into the Tigris.*
> *her tail he bent up into the sky to make the Milky Way,*
> *and her crotch he used to support the sky* (Baring and Cashford, p 278).

Many feminists become rightly distraught with this myth. It reflects violence towards women and may be seen as condoning rape and matricide. In more ancient myths, the Goddess divided by her own will, which was the God. In these myths, the God was an extension of the Goddess. He was the power by which she impregnated herself. In the above poem, the God appears separate from the Goddess. Yet, upon close inspection of the myth's beginning, it was Tiamant that generated Marduk for he was of her substance. (Lest Christians become self-righteous in judging such violence, let us recall the similar violence toward God of the crucifixion.)

As well as reflecting cosmic process, the myth of Tiamant and the biblical story reflect biological process. As discussed in the previous chapter, when a man's sperm dissolves into a woman's egg, she begins to divide and take form. Man is the initiator, or Eros, of woman's taking form as creation. In the above myth, Marduk is definitely fragmenting Tiamant; just as the Word fragments Tehom-Marie in the Bible. What is different in the myth of Marduk is his murderous attitude towards the Primordial Ocean. This attitude was not always the case in Babylonian myth. For example, consider the following writing from the same culture:

Marduk laid a reed upon the Face of the Waters. He formed dust and poured it out beside the reed. That He might cause the Gods to dwell in the habitation of their heart's desire. He formed mankind. The Goddess Aruru together with him created the seed of humanity. The beasts of the field and living creatures in the field he formed. (Baring and Cashford, 1991, p. 278).

What initiated the change from this type of writing to the one presented above? There are some historical explanations for this change, primarily centering on the invasion of matriarchal cultures that were agricultural in nature by patriarchal cultures that consisted of nomadic herdsmen. An excellent resource on this historical account is in Baring and Cashford's, *Myth of the Goddess: Evolution of an Image*.

Perhaps the conflict between farmers and cowboys in the modern musical, *Oklahoma*, is another version of the ancient story of conflict between herders and agriculturalists, between cultures based on yin and those based on yang. Are we, perhaps, looking at the source of dualism that perverts so much of modern thought in our culture of domination?

From a psychological point of view, perhaps the observation of natural process caused men to become fearful of women. Throughout the ancient world, the Goddess was the process of birth and death. The same womb that brought us into this life took us back, swallowing us whole. This may be why many "puritans" react negatively towards sex and discourage its occurrence. For example, there have been many religious sects who have suppressed the sexual power of women because they equated this power with death. This is why the *missionary position* (man on top) was the only sexual position sanctioned by the church for a long time. Man's domination of women equaled control of Nature and death.

FEAR OF NATURE, WOMEN, AND CHAOS

In today's world, this fear is manifested in our need to control nature with technologies. This is exemplified in genetic engineering and monoculture farming where individual differences and crop diversity are diminished. Just as our schools attempt to standardized education in the service of the factory and the military, our food production tries to stifle diversity in order to ensure control of life and, ultimately, quick profit. The fear that is behind this need to standardize is our fear of chaos or infinite potential. This is the ultimate uncertainty principle.

Our mass media hype fear of the weather and the wilderness, causing a run on the grocery chains whenever a storm is predicted and cutting us of from the forests and the "beasts". We destroy forests, rivers, waters, and air in pursuit of "civilization" and profit, with little thought given to the natural outcomes of such rape of Gaia. For many "civilized" people, zoos and circuses with their bars to protect us from the ferocity of wild animals and carefully groomed parks are their only exposure to nature. Not only do we cage the fearsome "beasts"; but also we cage ourselves "indoors," in boxed spaces. We heat and air-condition our indoor spaces to a very narrow temperature range, disempowering our ability to adapt and evolve with our changing natural environment. Many folks believe that some exposure to rain, cold, and wind—even our life-giving sun—makes us sick. Mother Culture keeps pounding such dreads into us, delaying our transcendence into our true relationship to Nature "out there" as well as our own true nature "in here." Even in our death, we are filled with chemicals and boxed into coffins, belying our true relationship to Mother Earth. God forbid, we should, in our turn, become food for the worms or push up daisies!

This fear of Nature's chaos further exposed itself in ancient myths where the female ate, dissolved, enveloped and enfolded the male within herself. The story of Gwion and Cerdwin is an excellent example, as is the story of Hansel and Gretel, the two children who almost get eaten by a witch. If we understood the metaphors of these stories, we would realize their linkage of eating to sex. These myths refer to the process of man being born of woman headfirst and his ultimate return to her headfirst through marriage, sex and death. Our language and our mythology unconsciously recognize this process. For example, the term *Mother* metaphorically relates to *mouth* (vaginas have lips and are the same basic shape), while the term *semen* derives from the Greek *sema*, meaning *seed and food*. Could this be the meaning behind the wearing of lipstick? The most popular color is red, symbolizing the blood of life.

107

The figure of the Egyptian Sky Goddess, Nut, swallowing and birthing the Sun God and Word, Ra in chapter 7 beautifully illustrates the process these words and practices describe. To understand this image, attend to your thoughts. They arise, they dance, and they return to the font of your mind. When you say an idea "dawned on me"; you are reflecting the birth of Ra from Nut. When you call someone's words, "food for thought"; you are reflecting Nut's absorption of Ra. Do you want to know your fate? Understand the image!

Various cultures throughout the world realize the Primordial Ocean Goddess as a Void, a Nothing or Darkness. It is interesting that this void is metaphorically equated to Water. Thus Genesis 1:2 states, "And the Earth was without form and void and darkness was upon the face of the deep." It is interesting that the name Marie means Ocean as evidenced by words like Marine and Marina. In many ways, then, the Virgin Birth is spoken to around the world and, even within the Bible may be spoken of in more than one way. For example, when the Word is made flesh in the New Testament's John 1:14, could it be that all the "Let there be" statements in Genesis 1, where what is spoken becomes. Is the New and Old Testaments speaking to the same process? Is this Virgin Birth of Marie a cosmic action on a personal level? I would even go far to state the Virgin Birth is the foundations of this moment of my writing and your reading. The Beginning of this Now is the Virgin!

For example, when the Buddhists speak of being unconditioned, we could say this is the Virgin Mind. Think of this in terms of how Christ was abused and ultimately crucified. If He became deconditioned of Roman-Jewish (add Christian and Muslim) rules and regulation; then the story of Jesus Christ reflects our story. IF we get the "balls" to become deconditioned (meaning beyond our conditioned mind), then are we not a threat? At this point, we become a threat to the "powers that be" and are open to abuse, imprisonment and execution on spiritual, psychological and physical levels.

Lao Tzu speaks to the process of the Virgin Birth beautifully in the *Tao Te Ching* when he says, *"be newborn, be free of yourself."* Being newborn *is* being free of yourself; i.e., your conditioned mind, or what you think you are. This is the Virgin Mind! How many newborns are virgins?

Think of the dangers in this state of mind!!!!

Yes, 20 years of schooling and you're going to toss it down the drain and challenge the system? Hey, you may find yourself hanging on a cross if you do so.

This popular Catholic Hymn, *Stella Maris, Star of the Sea,* expresses the universal insight:

Hail, Queen of heaven, the ocean star,
Guide of the wanderer here below,
Thrown on life's surge, we claim thy care,
Save us from peril and from woe.

Mother of Christ, Star of the sea
Pray for the wanderer, pray for me.

Moving over to the other side of the Atlantic, Speaking to the ocean, the Kogis, a South American indigenous tribe, sing:

In the beginning, there was only blackness.
Only the Sea.
In the beginning there was no sun, no moon, no people.
In the beginning there were no animals, no plants.
Only the Sea.
The Sea was the Mother.
The Mother was not people, She was not anything at all.
Nothing at all.

She was when She was, darkly.
(Harvey and Baring, 1995, p. 73)

Similarly, the Hindu sage, Ramprasad, gives us this poetry:

Treasures of revelation
emerge from the Mother Ocean...
Dive with abandon into her mystery.
You will discover a new gem every moment.
(Hixon, 1994, p. 53)

Also from the Hindu tradition, the *Rig Veda:* 10.129 sings:

There was neither non-existence nor existence then;
there was neither the realm of space not the sky which is beyond.
What stirred?
Where?
In whose protection?
Was there water, bottomless deep?

There was neither death nor immortality then.
There was no distinguishing sign of night nor of day.
That one breathed, windless, by its own impulse.
Other than that there was nothing beyond.
Darkness was hidden by darkness in the beginning;
with no distinguishing sign,
all this was Water.

The Life Force that was covered with emptiness,
that One arose through the power of heat.
Desire came upon that One in the beginning;
that was the first seed of Mind.
(Doniger, 1981, p. 25)

The dark Goddess, who also manifests as the Black Madonna of Eastern European Orthodox Christianity, is revealed in all her glory in these tributes from around the world.

Yet, many fear the void or darkness, believing it to represent non-existence. Indeed, one can hear our fear of this place through terms like *abysmal*. In the sense that the individual, isolated, and alienated self dies, these people are correct. However, in attending to the mystics of all traditions and to writings of physicists like David Bohm, one hears that this Abyss is infinite life, energy or consciousness. For example, in India, the name of the Abyss is *Ananta*. Imaged as a Serpent Goddess, her name means *endless*. *Ananta's* name unfolds experientially as the state of *Ananda*, meaning *Being, Consciousness and Bliss*. In Buddhist terms, this is Nirvana. The West calls this dissolution into the Absolute. In my terms, it is entering the Bridal Chambers.

In moving beyond our fears of the Abyss, listen to the following Hindu description of the Goddess Night:

The approaching Night, in her display, spreads over the twilight, which is but the reflected remnant of an apparent consciousness, itself but the veiling power of ignorance, of unconsciousness. It seems to us impossible that Night may ever entirely drive away Twilight, as well as all remnants of thought or perception, but the Absolute Night is the ultimate form of Consciousness and when perception of all appearances vanishes, she appears supremely resplendent. By comparison with her, Twilight and Dawn are but an obscurity. Just as Dawn vanishes when the Sun arises, so also the veiling power of ignorance dissolves when illumined by the Power of Consciousness. When the veiling power which appears to us as Light is consumed to his roots and previous deeds cease to bear consequences, then the non transcendent darkness which is the root of unknowing is forever destroyed.

This Goddess is one manifestation of the void and darkness of Genesis: 1:2; the Greek Nyx (Uncreated Night); and the modern day scientific evidence for dark matter (Danielou, 1991, p. 270)

In current times, there are many writings about the Dark Goddess. In the West, we approach her with fear and often deem her evil. Yet, the above meditation reveals the Dark Goddess as being infinite life in alignment with David Bohm's description of the Unmanifest as an Infinite Ocean of Energy. In my view, the Goddess is black because she is undifferentiated life. "I and Thou" are not two. In this state, there is nothing but the Goddess. She is without context. Experiencing this state is the divine marriage, for as we die in our orgasmic ecstasy, we are born into the Goddess in whom we lose our separate identity and achieve our full unity. Our lives are but a grooming for this special union. This is why men are *Bridegrooms*. A Bridegroom is one *groomed* for the enjoyment of the *Bride*.

Entering the bridal chambers of the Goddess entails getting naked with her. Our goal is to learn to become strippers so she can take delight in us and be revealed through us. There is a beautiful Pagan myth that states the Goddess, seeing herself in a mirror before the world became, fell in love with her reflection and kissed It. The mirror image fell away and eventually became male. When we get naked in the next chapter, we will discover ourselves as the Mother's mirror image. When we know ourselves as her mirror, we will experience that first kiss. What is more, we will realize it has been happening all the time.

As we move into Part 3 of this book, "Evolving Toward Wholeness," we will go deeper into these ideas by focusing on transcendence, not as an escape from the world, but as an embrace of all creation.

Part 3:
Evolving Towards Wholeness

Chapter 9
Transcendence Revisited
∽◯

You've got to go to Hell
Before you get to Heaven.
~ Steve Miller Band, Jet Airliner

What if death really *is* the portal to rebirth? What if Ken Wilber is right when he says, "In the manifest world, what we call 'matter' is not the lowest rung in the great spectrum of existence, but the exterior form of every rung in the great spectrum" (Wilbur, 2004). This means transcendence is not a matter of leaving the material world behind to enter some alternative heavenly kingdom, but of surrendering so totally to the here-and-now that we catch epiphanal glimpses of the infinite in the "here" and the eternal in the "now." Then the seemingly esoteric belief in transubstantiation of many Christians that bread and wine, received sacramentally, really *is* the Body and Blood of Christ is not so hard to grasp.

Transcendence is within our experiential realm right here, right now. Even the truly horrid experience of modern "news" may lead us to the awe-filled/awful awareness of our Earthly potential if we are willing to engage it rather than turn our back on it or defend against it. The impending end of available fossil fuel may yet transform us from grave robbers to midwives of Earth's energy. Perhaps the gift of this change will entail a return to Nature and our joyful participation in her bounty, if we can accept the loss of our current lifestyle mindfully. The loss of modern culture, as we have known her, may be the doorway that leads to deeper gain. Perhaps a new Earth will arise phoenix-like from the ashes.

PARABLE: BENSOPHIA
There is a parable that I wrote reflecting my spiritual process that speaks to this:

There once existed, in a land called Cuntainia in the tribe of Isis, a hard working young man of 13. His name was Bensophia. In those days, Bensophia was learning the craft of working with Nature by foraging through the forests with his father, Wilhelm, for nuts, berries, edible ferns and delightful fruits such as apples and pears growing plentifully wild upon the land. Being the age of 13, Bensophia was becoming a bit antsy because he had hoped to be soon earning his adult name. After all, it was custom for a young Isisian to become a man around the age of 13. Yet, it was up to Bensophia to determine how he would earn that name, and earn that name he felt he must, for he still was called his mother's son or Bensophia.

Bensophia lived amongst the Isisian peoples with his father, mother, 3 brothers and 3 sisters in the rich, fertile wilds of Cuntainia. In addition to foraging, he would help his father and older brother make various things from wood, while his oldest sister worked alongside their mother, tending the younger siblings and doing the work necessary for living such as preparing meals, telling stories, healing sicknesses and all those foundational feminine tasks.

One day, Bensophia was carving some wood while fantasizing about the ultimate receipt of his adult name. He became suddenly very ill. Seeing how pale his face was, his father told him to lie down under a Birch tree that was part of a forested lining between the village and the wild. Seeing the wisdom in his father's words, Bensophia took himself away from the village, towards the tree. But once he got there, something mysterious, the deafening voice of silence, called him deeper into the dark forested depths.

Taking a deep breath, he followed this voice. The silence there saturated Bensophia's ears. This silence was capped in an intense darkness resulting from the thick vegetation soaking up all the rays of the sun way above Bensophia's head. Yet, Bensophia took another deep breath and continued his walk.

Suddenly, Bensophia heard a hissing. Immediately, he realized that the sound was emanating from snakes. His face became flush and filled with sweat for snakes were his deepest fear. Frantically, he glanced around, scared of what he might find. But, he could not see the source of the hissing.

Frozen stiff in the dorm of his panic, Bensophia stood for what seemed an eternity. Yet, nothing happened. No snakes jumped up at him. Finally, he got up the nerve to move on. First, one step, then two. After the third step, he still saw no snakes. Cautiously, Bensophia took a few more steps. He then relaxed and began to walk. Then, all of a sudden, Bensophia heard a squeal emanate from his lips as he felt several sharp pains pulsating from his ankle. Cursing, he looked down to see 3 fleeing copperheads heading for the bushes. Bensophia realized he had been bitten and needed to take quick action before the poison of their bites took effect.

Blinded by a face full of sweat and feeling weak from sickness and fear, Bensophia's eyes fell upon a mighty Oak tree with sprouting roots across the forested dirt floor that would make a comfortable lining for him to sit and dig the poison out; and, that he did. However, just as he found a rock pointed enough to cut into his skin, Bensophia found himself falling asleep.

As his head nodded in drowsy drunkenness, Bensophia so longed for the scents of his sisters and brothers as they had lain next to him in their one room hut. Here in the woods, however, he had no such comfort. All that he smelled and heard were the scents and sounds of the forest enticing him to rest. Yet, he fought that rest, for he was afraid of letting go to the poison produced by the snakes. "What if a wild animal should eat me?" he thought. Beneath this explicit fear lay a deeper implicit one. He was petrified of letting go to eternal slumber.

Yet, his desire for sleep soon overtook him. As he drifted into a drowsy state of consciousness, he felt himself falling into a pit. This pit seemed never-ending and Bensophia realized he would be falling forever, for he was dying. Screaming, he held his hands above his head.

Falling faster and faster in what seemed to be eternity, the pangs of fear gripped Bensophia's pounding heart. Praying to the Great Mother, he suddenly realized he was flying. Soon, he realized the pit had transformed into the sky. "Ah", he thought, "I am on my way to Heaven."

Bensophia then discovered his body had disappeared. He was no longer a person and had become the wind! Sailing high, he then saw the mountains and the lakes that surrounded his village. He became amazed at how these appeared to make a pattern upon the sacred Earth. They all fit together into one tapestry. More than that, Bensophia saw how his life was part of that tapestry. Indeed, he found that not only was he part of the weaving of the landscape, but also was a part of the weaving of all human history and, indeed, the history of the entire planet and cosmos. Beyond that, he saw that all of these were woven within him. He was everywhere and always. Why Bensophia saw no beginning or end to himself in time or space.

Then, suddenly, quicker than the flash of an eye, Bensophia found himself in space. He saw that he was within the black brilliance of this space. This space was so intensely brilliant that it blinded Bensophia's eyes. This brilliance was a great beauty, a mysterious Presence more powerful than anything he had ever known. There was no end to the power. Bensophia was within what seemed to outshine all the stars in the universe. Indeed, the brilliance of this dark blotted out the Sun. He realized he was in the womb of the Great Mother.

Suddenly, Bensophia's attention was drawn to the blue Earth shining forth her radiant glory below his feet. Tears formed in his eyes from the sight for there was no place he was not embracing. Bensophia felt a powerful energy circulating through his body. Every cell appeared to be on fire. Bensophia screamed in the agony of joy, knowing he was still alive.

He then awoke under the Oak tree. "Fate has spared me," he mumbled to the forest in a drowsy haze. Bensophia then lay back on the tree to recuperate. "I'm such a lucky man," he thought.

When he got his energy back, Bensophia got up and began to walk towards the family hut lying on the outskirts of the village.

In that walk home, he felt something new had been born within him. It was more than his being in the Great Mother. He suddenly realized she was within him and that his collapse into death was a collapse into his Self.

*As such, Bensophia realized he was not walking back to the farm as the same boy. He further realized his special name **was** Bensophia and he knew the deep meaning of the name given to him at birth. Bensophia realized himself a man, for he had been reborn. The snakes had fathered that emergence within him. For that, he sent prayers of deep gratitude out into the universe and deep into his heart.*

At some point, the adolescent needs to become like Bensophia and earn his manhood by finding his source of power within himself. Ultimately each adolescent needs to develop a sense that the "locus of control" lies within himself, so that his labors too can be fruitful.

Bensophia's story depicts a rite of passage sadly lacking in our culture. The bites of the three snakes are the calls of his primal energy that ultimately kill him as the child he has always known himself to be. This death by snakebite leads his Soul into transcendent ecstasy. His story further speaks to the labor of childbirth, of unfolding a potential that lies within us, that is initiated by going into the pits. Within all of us lies infinite potential waiting to be born. Indeed, each moment could be seen as the unfolding of potential, as well as our reaction to it. Each moment, then, is labor, for each moment is a production.

Just as Eternity gives birth to each moment, so does each moment give birth to Eternity. We live and move and have our being in one never-ending Mobius loop where interior and exterior are continuous.

GIVING BIRTH

In the maternal delivery room, there are various approaches to dealing with the pain of labor. The first is to suppress the pain. Those that espouse medication or teach techniques that take attention away from the pain and place it somewhere else (e.g., Lamaze) are examples of those that suppress the pain. The second way is to not deal with the situation all. Examples of this would be epidurals or C-sections. The third way is to go into the pain. Some women who have gone into the pain have described transcendental experiences such as the marrying of pain and joy or great sexual pleasure replacing pain. Just as sitting atop a mountain allows you to see the surrounding landscape patterns, going into the pain allows you to get a more holistic perspective that integrates seemingly opposing feelings.

Then, there is a fourth way of childbirth, a more ancient way. That way is both primal and transcendent. The mother surrenders entirely to the creative forces of the universe moving through her. The question of pain becomes irrelevant. The process simply IS. My stepdaughter, Jessica, experienced this path with her last child, Skye. This is an ancient way for women of the past (and in some current traditional cultures) who would give birth while working in the fields or foraging in the forest. More than a conscious way, though, this is about how the labor process is experienced and raises the question, "do our labors have to be so painful?"

This question is brought out in the Bible's Book of Genesis where Eve is cursed to labor in pain because she ate the fruit of knowledge, the apple. The apple is an important fruit spiritually because it reflects Wisdom herself. If you cut an apple in cross sections, its seeds make a 5-point pentagram, an ancient symbol for the Goddess and reflective, interestingly, of how the orbit of Venus appears to us on Earth. It is also inherent in the Leonardo da Vinci "Vitruvian Man," whose spread out legs and arms coupled with his head make a 5 - point star. It is well known by esoterics of various disciplines that da Vinci had dabbled in the mystical arts.

Once the apple opened our primal parents' eyes, they interestingly became ashamed of their being naked. There are many interpretations to this act and each interpretation is correct in relation to the person taking in the words. My interpretation is that our Parents (i.e., the ancients) had developed an ego-consciousness that said their beauty was "bad."

Ultimately, God becomes angry that they are ashamed and banishes them from paradise. Many current ecopsychologists interpret this banishment to reflect a historical movement from the more laid-back lifestyles of hunting and gathering societies which some call the original society of leisure. Most indigenous peoples that live wild work on the average of four hours per day and spend the rest of the time telling stories, socializing over food preparation and so on.

As punishment for eating the fruit, God sends Adam and Eve out of Paradise and makes their labors hard. If we follow the lifestyles of the ancient hunting and gathering societies, then our hard labor came about due to farming. Lord Jesus gave the basic same message about labor when He says in Matthew 6:28-29:

Consider the lilies of the field, how they grow; they neither toil nor spin, yet I tell you, even Solomon in all his glory was not arrayed like one of these.

Allowing one's self to work with Nature and do Nature's bidding entails living a life free of toil. Of course, that doesn't mean deathless, but it does mean being a part of the process of death and the recreation it sparks. The dead lily in the winter becomes the fertilizer for new life in the spring. Death is a living process. Knowing this is eternal life.

The Biblical book of Genesis says, "Be fruitful and multiply." This statement is about much more than having babies and populating the world. It is also about our labors as we give birth to all that is within us. Labor involves going into the process, pain and all, and creating joyfully. It involves going into our darkness and birthing what is hidden. For example, my writings often appear to come out of nowhere. After their birth, I form them for proper presentation by editing and having others edit, as my wife is doing with this book. Loving hands and minds help bring what comes out raw from my Soul's womb to maturity. These are my "labors of love." Indeed, all our labors should be this way.

TRANSFORMING OUR VIEW OF DARKNESS
Rumi talks about going into the darkness beautifully in the following poem:

> Bend like the limb of a peach tree
> Tend those who need help.
> Disappear three days with the moon.
>
> Don't pray to be healed or look for evidence
> Of some other world.
> You are the Soul
> And medicine for what wounds the Soul."
> (1997, p. 48)

To bend like the limb of a peach tree is to flow with your pain or other feelings, not struggle against them. When the wind blows, go with it so you don't break. In response to a recent storm, the birch trees surrounding our home bowed over until their heads touched the ground. Their humility created a beautiful bower through which our spirits were invited to walk. As the sun arose, the ice that coated each branch became multiple prisms, shining forth all the colors of the rainbow. Then as it melted, the birches stood erect again, pointing upward to the sun that had anointed them.

Rumi further advises us to go into the dark. *"Disappear three days with the moon."* We must bow down to that which is greater than ourselves. It is this dark that we are most afraid to go into; yet it is in not confronting this dark that we stay stuck. Like Bensophia, we have to explore the dark silence of our inner wilderness. Ultimately, we'll find that our fears make it seem worse than it really is. (The exception to this principle is when the suffering comes from some horrid condition imposed willfully by others, such as rape or torture. The mindsets of the perpetrators of such atrocities are based on control and domination, not on empowering the other person through Love. It is only such perversions of the natural, cyclical rather than hierarchical order that necessarily cause suffering.)

Rumi tells us that we *are* the medicine that heals us. Think of your pain as a planet. If you try to escape its gravitational pull, you will find yourself in orbit around it and will remain stuck. The gravitational pull of the pain and your resistance, interact in such a way that you cannot escape. The pain pulls you in while you try to pull away, setting up a situation akin to a spaceship trying to escape the Earth at a certain speed while the Earth is trying to bring it back down. This is how satellites and spaceships go into orbit. Do we want the same situation with our pain? Just as the spaceship is stuck in orbit around the Earth, you will be under the control of the pain.

However, if you go into the pain, you will find yourself going through it and emerging renewed. You will discover that pain is your friend or teacher. It warns you that something within you needs to be transformed and inspiring you to find the courage and wisdom necessary for such transformation. You will experience transcendence, a rebirth.

Imagine childbirth. A child emerges between shit and piss. We think these disgusting, and some early Christians saw this condition as reflecting our disgrace before God. Yet, as any farmer will tell you, plants don't grow without the rich, fertilizing power of shit and decay. That which our minds see as disgusting and filthy, flowers see as God's gift. William Butler Yeats expresses this thought in poetry:

> But love has pitched his mansion in
> The place of excrement
> For nothing can be sole or whole
> That has not been rent.

Perhaps we too can see the shit that falls upon us as God's gift. Perhaps in our Ground, that dark, rich Mother from which we spring, shit allows us to emerge and open our petals to the loving touch of the sun's rays. Perhaps it is further telling that some women teasingly call their children their "little turds." Perhaps the children produced by their mothers' bodies are indeed the fruits that bring forth new life. In that statement is our hope for the future. May all our children be our "little turds"!

In today's world, we are confronted with many issues that can be seen as shit. We are at the visible end of our oil resources. Our politics is revealing a lot of corruption and oppression. There is an increasing divide between the rich and the poor. While the economy is said to be in good shape, that good shape is defined by how the stock market is going. In other words, it is being defined by the conditions of the upper class and is not taking into account information like health care costs for the middle class and poor. Furthermore, our health is being put at risk by unsafe farming practices. For example, there is a growing use in agribusiness of destructive monoculture that depletes the soil and ultimately affects our health through the production of foods laden with chemicals at best and genetically engineered at worse.

These dangers have reached an apex. We are on the brink of a precipitous fall. The good news is that this does not have to end in a horror story. Going into the issues and confronting them can lead to a more holistic life. Such movements as non-violent resistance, eco-village living, biodynamic farming, and permaculture are showing the way. These alternatives return us to our true nature. For instance, in permaculture a variety of plants grow together in "guilds", synergistically supporting one another, the farmer, and the ecosystem. We can bring forth the *Promised Land* that is a common theme in the Bible and indeed most religious teachings throughout the world.

THE STAR OF DAVID

The Star of David reflects the process of descent into hell in order to ascend to heaven. The downward pointing triangle of this star reflects the necessary descent, such as the slavery experienced by the Jews in Egypt, the crucifixion of Jesus and the turmoil in the beginning of the Book of Revelation.

The upward pointing triangle, then, is about transcendence, leading us up the Cosmic Mountain where all is revealed, exemplified by the ascent of Moses onto Mount Sinai, the resurrection of Christ, or the marriage of Jesus to New Jerusalem or Peace. Bensophia's rite of passage illustrates the integration of these seemingly opposite movements of descent and ascent.

Understanding the individual stories of the Bible as being one, some mystical Christians feel that Adam is the fallen "Man", while Jesus is the resurrection. Adam is the downward pointing triangle, and Jesus is the upward. They are ultimately one Man just as the multitude of stories included in the scriptures becomes revealed as one story. In this view, the whole body of myths, stories, poetry, art and science unites us in one story. Hence, Bensophia sees himself in the tapestry of the entire world. The Bible is not about a story separate from us. It and other spiritual teachings reveal us! They are *our* life story, here, now and always. We carry Adam-Moses-Jesus-Buddha-Mohammad in our genes and in our stories. In relationship to the *teachings*, we are all strippers revealing our true Essence, which is God, Allah, The Great Spirit, Gaia or, in my case, Sophia.

What is in the big story reflected in the Bible is within our culture at large and within us. This is the true Gospel or Good News. What is microscopic is macroscopic. All scriptures are not about times past. They transcend time. They are about you and me here and now. Rather than history, it is *ourstory*.

Indeed, we are at a point now where the "shit" that is happening in the world can be seen as a God's gift. We must enter into that shit consciously, as the Gestalt therapists teach. We must place ourselves on the cross of Christ or make the painful climb up Mount Sinai after leaving slavery behind us. We can enter a brighter day that transcends this one. We can become the one groomed for the Bride, i.e., *Jerusalem* or our *Place of Peace*.

We can transcend our current cultural conditions and move into brighter days. Just as Moses led the Jews out of slavery and into the glory of God, we too can be led out of our slavery into a system in which all creatures are free. Understand that Moses is a force moving us today, not just in times past. Ultimately, transcendence is about transcending institutional boundaries of Christian, Muslim, Pagan, Hindu or Jew. Such designations do not matter, for the spirit of Moses, his genes and his wisdom are always within all those groups.

For us in the so-called civilized cultures, transcendence is about moving beyond our current addictions to possessions, hierarchical status, and superficial relationships and into the freedom of loving freely in the true nakedness of our being. Babies are born naked and are conceived in their parent's nakedness. So too, in our nakedness, we will see the glory of God radiate from within us. All we have to give up is shame, not by escaping it, but by descending into it to discover the true beauty of our inner darkness which will burst upwards like spring flowers, transporting us to new heights of creativity and Love. Like the birches, we must let go of arrogant ego and bow down to the greater power that enfolds and upholds us. Then we can raise our heads, our hands, and our voices in celebration and service.

To take this process to a higher level, the next chapter deals with ecstasy in Nature. By allowing one's self to be seduced by her, one finds one's self entering into ecstasies that ultimately are more powerful than all the shining suns in the universe.

Chapter 10
Ecstasy and Nature

‿◦⁀

Drive me out of my mind, O Mother!
What use is esoteric knowledge or philosophical
discrimination? Transport me totally with the burning
wine of your all-embracing Love. Mother of
Mystery, who imbues with mystery those who love you,
immerse irretrievably in the stormy ocean without
boundary, pure Love, pure Love, pure Love.
~ Ramprasad quoted in Hixon, 1994

I often venture into the woods to rejoice and participate in Nature. She is my church. The scant remains of the wild serve as a refuge from the day-to-day rat race of suburban living. It helps me to bond with my spiritual lover, Gaia, the body of Nature.

The entire body of Nature is mine to explore and love. She is my home. All it takes to make love with her is an open mind and an ability to get out of my head. In the woods, I love to walk about and absorb the textures, smells, and sensations of the Great Goddess. The feel of the caressing air, coupled with the smell of flowers and trees, generates peace of mind and solitude. In this state, I know myself as child and lover. The smells, tastes, and enveloping dampness of the air and Earth are a return to the warmth and comfort of the womb. Such ecstatic experiences in nature may be rare, but when I open myself to Nature and attend patiently, they do come.

In Nature I am wealthy. The sun and the moon spread an expanse of sparkling diamonds across the waters or the snow. All with eyes to see share in this wealth. No exotic jewelry, designed only for the elite, can come anywhere near it beauty. Nature enriches the most humble beyond measure.

This synopsis of experiences with Nature is about merging with Sophia's daughter, Ecstasy. I consider her synonymous with Sophia for she always shouts words of joy in all her creations. In my relationship to Nature, I can be both son and lover, just as the primal Word and Desire are both in all the creation stories, without perversion or pathology. My relationship to Nature is a holographic image, a sacrament, or a temporal manifestation of my eternal relationship to Sophia. In my ecstatic intercourse with Nature, I am gifted with visceral, non-intellectualized evidence that God and Nature are one. Moreover, I am related to him/her by inalienable bonds of Love, thus I am also one with God and Nature. We are a Divine Trinity, as mysterious and paradoxical yet true as the Trinity familiar to the orthodox Christian.

When we humans go deep inside ourselves in contemplation, we know no distinction between Self, Nature, and Divinity. We see ourselves in the starry heavens and the dirt of the Earth. Nature mirrors us as we mirror her. Just as the beautiful colors of the sunset sky are reflected in the waters of the bay, giving them a beauty beyond utterance, so too, they are reflected in our hearts, giving us peace. "As above; so below!"

It has been said many times the world over that by connecting to the natural we find ourselves. For example, a traditional Navajo chant goes:

The mountain, I become it.
The herb, the fir tree, I become it.
The morning mist, the cloud, the gathering water, I become it.
The wilderness, the dewdrop, the pollen, I become it.

When we enter these connected states of mind, we find our kinship in Nature and know our infinity. We are not separate from the environment. Goethe taught us, "a mode of interaction between people and environment that involves reciprocity, wonderment, and gratitude." (Seaman, 1998). He wished us to encounter nature respectfully and to discover how all its parts, including ourselves, belong. In this way, perhaps, we come to feel more care for the natural world, which answers back with meaning. Alan Watts (1995) tells us truly:

You didn't come into this world. You came out of it, like a wave from the ocean. You are not a stranger here.

Just as Nature is our true Mother and our spiritual teacher, she is also our bride. When we become ready to marry her in our hearts, she allows us to lift the bridal veil that has hitherto concealed spiritual Truth from us. Where before we had seen only the beauty of Nature, we now see the face of Sophia. She reveals to us the divine nature of our earthly home and teaches us that we also provide a home for divinity within our hearts. She unveils the truth that we are interactive with God and Nature, and then (wonder of wonders!) goes even deeper into the mystery of our being.

Lifting the bridal veil also reveals the groom as one with his bride. We are her husband and also his wife! When the groom lifts his beloved's veil, he is gazing metaphorically into the eyes of his own true Nature, his essence or truth, which is, ultimately, the ground of being from which he sprang. Each human being is one among many diverse manifestations of God/Nature. We are all revealed as one at heart: male and female, mountain and cave, Heaven and Earth, God and humanity, Sophia and Nature–all One.

THE DANCE OF THE SEVEN VEILS: IN SEARCH OF ECSTASY

As progressive veils are stripped from our true nature in the intimacy of marriage, we reach a depth of Nature that is unnamed and unnamable. Thought cannot penetrate or divide her. The purity of her essence is so absolute that it cannot be contained, contaminated, or contemplated. She is eternally virgin. Everything I say about this Nature is false! One cannot speak of or comprehend her in any form or fashion. She is unthinkable and incomprehensible. In this, I only wish to provide the reader with some ways to unite with and experience her. I do not wish to give the impression I have grasped the ungraspable. Every approximation of Truth that we can state intellectually and verbally is false, for comprehension entails limitations on the illimitable. All theories are dim shadows of the great IAM or ISIS.

It is only in the dim and reflected light of my false notion of Nature as essence, that I say Nature is ecstasy. This is as close as I can come to a holographic representation of the Truth. Just as manmade jewelry, however beautiful, is but a dim reflection of living light dancing on virgin snow, so too are our words a dim reflection of Truth. The term *Ecstasy* is from the Greek *Ekstasis*, meaning *to stand forth naked* (Walker, 1983, p. 269). It is a term that signifies a state of mind that emerges in a religious trance, when one is able to strip away the surface self, leaving only the essential self or consciousness.

As the name *Ecstasy* implies, we would all do well to learn the art of striptease. This dance is ancient and its original function was spiritual. Ancients called it the *Dance of the Seven Veils.* Each veil was a representation of a surface layer of Nature. When the dancer removed the last veil, the witness beheld Truth in all her naked glory. This dance is our human, temporal representation of divine, eternal Nature as Essence.

To remove these surface veils, we have to become metaphorical dancers, ridding ourselves of ourselves. We must become like Inanna descending to meet her sister, Ereshkigal, the queen of the underworld. We must divest ourselves of and surrender all vestments and vestiges of rank and pride. All ideas about who we think we are must go, surrendered to the Divine Nature. We then become an imagination infinite in its ability to conceive. Christian mystic, Jan van Ruysbroeck, illustrates this idea clearly:

> *Could we renounce ourselves and all selfhood in our works, we should, with our bare imageless Spirit, transcend all things and without intermediary we should be led by the Spirit into the Nudity. When we renounce ourselves and become, in our ascent towards God, so simple that the naked Love in the height can lay hold of us, where Love enfolds Love, above every exercise of virtue - that is, in our Origin, of which we are spiritually born - then we cease and we and all our selfhood die in God. And in this death we become hidden Sons of God and find a new Life within us, and that is Eternal Life.* (Iyer, 1988, p. 450)

Many people mistakenly believe transcending all things means to deny the world. This idea is not true. Transcendence entails the destruction of the illusion that there is an objective world "out there," with a subjective person "in here." Transcendence requires an embrace of the world, akin to my experiences in Nature. Each "image" we hold of ourselves is but another veil to be discarded. Each image of ourselves is an idol that must be smashed.

As illustrated by van Ruysbroeck, our naked Spirit is imageless. The Spirit or Soul is without form, without taste, without anything at all. It is akin to the universe before creation, "without form and void" (Genesis I). In our naked Spirit, we have no ideas about the world or ourselves. In this state, the world and the Spirit are one. When we strip and expose our bare core, we become like a man who loses all sense of himself in transcendent ecstasy upon immersing himself in his lover's vagina. What is within is without and what is without is within. The Hindu *Chhandogya Upanishad* (7.25.I-2 abridged) beautifully summarizes the transcending and unifying powers of Ecstasy:

> *It is above, it is below, it is to the west, it is to the east, it is to the south, it is to the north: It is, in fact, this entire world.*
>
> *And truly, the one who sees this, thinks this, and understands this, takes pleasure in the Self, is joined to the Self, knows bliss in the Self: such a one is autonomous. He has unlimited freedom in all worlds. But those who think otherwise than this are ruled by others, inhabit perishable worlds, and in all worlds are unfree.*(Campbell, 1974, p. 54)

These words contain the essence of healing: becoming whole, at one with our nature again. Moreover, they contain the essence of lovemaking, allowing self and other to merge. Such experiences are the birthright of all beings on Earth. They are the source of Ecstasy, engendering health, joy, and procreativity, both for us and for our planet. The

Self of which this Upanishad is speaking is completely non-conceived or uncreated. Yet, this non-conceived Self is the conceiver of all things. Where is this non-conceived conceiver? According to contemplator, Wei Wu Wei, she is what is looking!

> *What is the use of looking outside? All you will see is objects!*
> *Turn around and look within.*
> *Shall I then see Subject instead?*
> *If you did you would be looking at an object. An object is such in whatever direction you look.*
> *Shall I not see myself?*
> *You cannot see what is not there!*
> *What, then, shall I see?*
> *Perhaps you may see the absence of yourself, which is what is looking. It has been called the Void...The Void is what you can't see when you are looking for a self that isn't there. Why is that? Because it is what is looking.*(Wilber, 1993, p. 321)

FINDING OUR TRUE NATURE

Chasing after one's nature is similar to a dog chasing its own tail. Nature is ungraspable. Could we possibly reach out and pick up one of those diamonds that dance upon the water? Can we walk upon that pathway we perceive laid out by the moon and leading directly to our individual hearts? Only when we allow our egos to dissolve into our Christ consciousness! Trying to grasp your nature is like trying to grasp the horizon. You can walk forever towards it in an attempt to grasp it. However, you can never reach it. It is always the same distance ahead of you. Yet, upon awakening, you discover that you are already there; have always been there; and will always be there!

In the Godhead, all is wholeness. Subject and object are married as one. Say "I, me, you, we, us, he, him, she, her, they, or them"; it matters not, for it is all the same. Vocabulary and grammar dissolve into the great (w)hole!

How do we get to experience this virgin purity of Nature? Matthew Fox (1981), spiritual contemplator and founder of *The Institute for Creation Spirituality*, distinguishes between two primary ways of experiencing ecstasy: natural and tactical. The primary difference between the two is that natural ecstasy is an end in itself, while tactical ecstasy is a means towards the end. I like to think of natural ecstasy as being spontaneous, in that the lover sees the ecstasy as "accidental." Such a natural ecstasy occurred, for instance, when my wife and I were sitting on a tiny beach behind a huge rock cliff and were surprised/ delighted/transformed by a huge wave that overtopped the cliff, threatening to drench us. In that delicious instant, we experienced our oneness with our surroundings. Awareness of our vulnerability to the great forces of Nature married horror with joy within us. We turned toward each other with exuberant laughter, far beyond verbalization. Only later could we discuss how fear, delight, and awe converged in that ecstatic instant.

Tactical ecstasy, in contrast, is a practice, such as meditation or ritual that *might* lead to a natural ecstasy. Kundalini practices are tactical ecstasy that may or may not implode into natural ecstasy. Rousing your energy, putting on your coat and boots, and getting out there in the woods on an early cold morning is tactical ecstasy. It is the spiritual and physical discipline through which you make yourself available to Ecstasy. Most of the time, I am not even seeking a powerful mystical experience. I am just looking for some quiet time to myself. Then, an ecstasy happens without my asking. The sweet perfumes of Nature overtake me, and I experience bliss. Such experiences are a grace or a blessing, not an automatic reward for good behavior. We simply can engage ourselves in the tactics and hope that Nature will bless us by sweeping us away in her own ecstatic passion.

Both of these paths lead to realization of our unity in the Godhead. However, they do not lead to a *grasping* of the Godhead, who is Truth. Egyptian Goddess, Isis, reflects this great and paradoxical mystery when she states mortal men cannot unveil her. As an eye cannot behold itself, Isis is never seen naked by men because she is the Seer of men and the Seer cannot see herself.

Some ancient cultures believed a man would die if he saw the Goddess naked. The reason he dies is that the Goddess naked is the Seer. In his death or surrender, the man dissolves into the Seer and awakens as her, just as a mouse awakens as a cat upon being devoured. At the deepest level mystery and awe blow away all pretense and vanity. We return to the singular indefinable infinity whence we emerged.

Consider these ideas through the lens of the following Egyptian poem presented in Baring and Cashford (1991, p. 255):

> *My majesty precedes me as Ihy, the Sun of Hathor*
> *I am the Male of Masculinity,*
> *I slid forth from the outflow between her thighs*
> *in this my name of Jackal of the Light.*
> *I broke forth from the egg. I oozed out of Her Essence,*
> *I escaped in her blood. I am the master of the redness.*
> *I am the Bull of Confusion, my Mother Isis generated me*
> *though she was ignorant of herself.*

The view of Isis as ignorant of herself does not mean she is a stupid Goddess. It means she is Infinity. The Infinite cannot exist side-by-side with herself. Hence, she cannot behold herself because there is nothing within her but she within herself. She is without context. For Isis to be aware of herself, there has to be a context: an "I and Thou"; an "Ihy and an Isis"; an "Infinite and a Finite," or a "Thinker and a Thought."

SOURCE OF EVIL
Thought has a tendency to turn what is Absolute Subject into an object. This alchemy is, of course, blasphemy! In this sense all utterance, all language, with its distinctions of vocabulary and grammar, is blasphemous...perhaps, even, original sin!

Within this intrinsic riddle may lie the elusive reason for evil in the manifest world. The wonder of creation necessarily entails the horror of duality and destruction. Love entails alienation or there is no Other to love. Only when we recognize death as an intrinsic, inevitable part of life's cycle does it lose its sting. This riddle is certainly why the world universally sees the Word as a dividing principle or a power that fragments life. For example, in the bible's Book of Proverbs: 8:27, the Word is said to place a compass on the Deep, measuring out that which is immeasurable.

Thought places boundaries on the Infinite and generates a sense of "I and Thou." Thought generates context. When observed the wave becomes a particle. We can only participate in the active wave; we cannot observe it. Newton honored and observed the beautiful butterfly by crucifying it. Meister Eckhart presents this idea when he writes, "*All is unity in the Godhead and cannot be spoken of*" (Fox, 1995, p. 34). This means the Godhead is beyond thought and indivisible by thought. Eckhart goes on to say, "*When I flow forth from There, all creatures shout God!*" This means that once thought flows from the depths of God, a context is created. She is divided into an I and a Thou. (I, the writer, you, the reader, and the language of this text all become possible, indeed inevitable.) In the Godhead, creatures exist in unity and have no sense of God or themselves. They exist in That-in-which-there-is-no-other. Hence, the Godhead is unspeakable because there is no context in her.

Eckhart's words imply *we* are the Uncreated in our ground. When Ihy emerges from the outflow between the thighs of Isis, Meister Eckhart emerges right along with him. Again, as Eckhart states:

> *In my birth, all things were born and I was the cause of myself and all things...and if I had not been, then God had not been either.*
> (Campbell, 1974, p. 64)

If you try to grasp all this, you will lose it. Once you stop trying to grasp Ecstasy, you will find yourself married to her. Such is the mystical trance. Such is bliss. This is why you are a *Bridegroom*, regardless of your biological gender. On your honeymoon night, Ecstasy will devour you. When Ecstasy overtakes you, you return to the Godhead. This is your awakening.

Ecstasy is a devouring Goddess. In being devoured, we disperse throughout her body as food disperses throughout the body of the consumer. Dissolution in Ecstasy is not death as we fear it, but rather the death that leads to our resurrection, like a phoenix. In her, death is part of the life-death-rebirth cycle, not finality. Do not be afraid of Ecstasy's cooking pot. Hop right in.

To the ancient Greek way of thinking, becoming Ecstasy's meal is one's awakening as Zoë, meaning Infinite Life. (Baring and Cashford, 1991) Where may we find Zoë? Nowhere! Zoë is not locatable because she is the Seer and Conceiver of these words as reader and writer who can neither see nor conceive herself. Try to find your Consciousness or your Wisdom somewhere in the brain. Try to locate your soul in your body. Bet you cannot do it! She is not here, nor is she there. Yet, she is what is looking. This is why the term *nowhere* opens into now-here. We exist and think, write and read this book, within the apostrophe. Zoë is the eternally now-here non-conceived Conceiver. She is the Unmanifest or Uncreated. Who is this Uncreated Creator? Your very own Spirit or Soul!

In the next chapter, we will go deeper into ancient ideas on the uncreated Goddess by examining her history. We will further unfold a web revealing the women of the Bible to be various manifestations of Sophia Herself.

Chapter 11
The Tangled Web We Weave
⌒♡

Oh, what a tangled web we weave
When first we practice to deceive
~ Sir Walter Scott

Napoleon once said, "History is a lie agreed upon." This is true. There is no verifiable and objective history "out there" independent of the historian. We have been taught a paternalistic, militarized version of *his*-story that totally distorts *her*-story, consigning it to heresy. The "winner" gets to write history, and for the last four thousand years, patriarchal warriors have been the evident winners. History is a function of the historian just as the physical manifestation of an electron as particle or wave is a function of whether or not a scientist is looking. Our accounting of history is not so much about trying to find objective facts as it is about reflecting our inner workings manifested as values, passions and prejudices. This is why our elementary history classes focus so much on wars and violent revolutions. They reflect the mindset of a culture that idolizes dominance, control, and violence. (Just watch an afternoon of after-school cartoon if you don't believe me.) History, as we have been taught it, deceives us about the nature of the Goddess, women, and humanity at large.

Is there a more peaceful way to look at history? Some modern feminist thinkers, such as Riane Eisler (1996), believe so. The primary reason that this feminist history resonates with me is because it reflects how my mind sees the Goddess, in both human and cosmic form. When I vowed to marry Athena as a pubescent boy, this proposal was more than a childish fantasy. My commitment to Athena is seen in the work I am doing on this book. As a man might send flowers to reflect his love for his lady, this book is a reflection of my love and devotion to Sophia-Athena. Most importantly, in this childhood experience was my reasoning that Athena was a woman/Goddess because I perceived the function of Wisdom as conceiving thought. In other words, everything I present in this book, including the research, is not about independently verifiable evidence. Rather, everything I present is because I feel the information in my guts and it is in this fact that I say it is true.

If some read this work and say it's "bullshit," then that idea is *in their minds* and for them is true. However, this work being "bullshit" is not objective fact. It is subjective impression. For others, this work will ring true and it will inspire them. Those who like this work and those who dislike it do so because of their own processing, values, and prejudicial stances. What would create peace in this world would be for us to realize this subjectivity of perception and develop respect for the various outlooks on this world. Ultimately, they all unite as one. The motto for the United States is *E Pluribus Unum,* meaning, *Unity in Diversity.* This statement moves beyond the political nation and reveals the United States (a plurality of consciousnesses in unison) as the condition of all humanity in the God/Goddess.

With that said, I do hope this helps me to connect with women and men who can see the feminine as reflections of cosmic power and, ultimately, their own creative power or what the Hindus call *Shakti*. I also hope these words help support a movement that moves beyond the modern day cognitive stance of needing dominance and control, manifesting, instead, a realization of the partnership between the sexes, all of humanity, the entire planetary ecosystem, and, indeed, the living Cosmos.

In *Charlotte's Web*, the spider, Charlotte, spins into her web the words that save the pig she eulogizes. Though the pig gets all the notoriety, Charlotte is the true, though unsung hero. (White, 1952) Similarly, the Goddess is a true, though devalued hero of the human story. She is the power and principle behind the creation of a thought, a developing embryo, and the entire cosmos.

My primary belief is that the Goddess is the power by which all are born, maintained, and dissolved. It is she who weaves the entire web of life. During the Greco-Roman period, the dividing impulse of man separated these three powers of the feminine and treated them as if they were three distinct beings. An image of a young woman would represent the Goddess as the Virgin; a birth-giving matron would represent her as the Mother; and an old woman would represent her as dissolution into timeless life. Dividing these powers out is important so that we can see how they operate. Unfortunately, the drawback is that we cannot see the wholeness of the process, for we don't see the wholeness of the Goddess.

Some contemporary authors argue this type of dualistic thinking resulted from the Greco-Roman civilization being at the beginning of the *Age of Pisces*. The sign for Pisces is two fish swimming away from one another, an obvious symbol of dualistic thinking. In this dualistic "push me-pull you" mindset, we weave a tangled web indeed. According to these contemplators, we are now on the threshold of entering the *Age of Aquarius*. The symbol for this age is the *Water Bearer*, a metaphor for the Depths and indivisible Life. As discussed, Water is also linked to the ancient Goddess (e.g., Genesis 1:2). Perhaps we will see things more holistically again.

DENUNCIATION OF THE GODDESS

Throughout the patriarchal ages, many of the terms once used to denote the Goddess have been turned into symbols for evil. This has polluted the sacredness of womanhood. For example, the common term used to denote an evil old woman is *Hag*. This is not a term originally used to denounce mean and nasty women living in the autumn of their years. Instead, the term emanates from the Greco-Roman *Hagia*, meaning *Holy* (Walkers, 1983, p. 366). This term originally referred to God's Wisdom in the Eastern Christian mosque, *The Hagia Sophia* (Walkers, 1983). *Hagia* is a cognate to the Egyptian *Heq* and refers to an ancient matriarch who knew words of power or could perform magical rites. Similarly, the Hebrew name for Sophia, *Hockhmah*, unfolds from the Egyptian *Heq-Maa* or *Heka-Maat* (Walkers, 1983).

The Virgin, Mother, and Hag trio were not three separate women in pre-Roman Latin. Instead, they were under the collective name of *Uni*, meaning *the One*. This name is a cognate to the Oriental *Yoni* and refers to the genitals of women while meaning *place of rest and to unite* (Walkers, 1983). The threefold functions of the Yoni (birth, sustenance, absorption) entail the essence of the Creative Process. The Hindu Saint, Ramakrishna, poetically describes this Process below:

> *More than Creator and creation,*
> *Mother is pure Creativity*
> *beyond any notion of duality.*

Universe and Father-God
Are thrilling glances from her seductive eyes.
Always pregnant with Ecstasy,
She gives birth to manifest Being
From her womb of primordial Awareness,
nursing him tenderly at her breast,
She playfully consumes her child.
The world dissolves instantly
upon touching her white teeth,
attaining the realization of
her brilliant and translucent void.
(Hixon, 1992, p. 204)

Another term used to destroy the sacredness of women is *pussy.* Human men and boys often use this term as an insult towards another male. Its usage entails an attack on one's manhood by considering him female. Likewise, the common term *sissy* is from the same root as sister. In these attacks, being considered a pussy or sissy is identical to being considered inferior. The terms also serves as crude references to a woman's genitals and a woman's entire being.

Without insulting the reader's intelligence and knowledge of the English language, the term *pussy* also refers to a *cat.* The question is how did women become associated with this great huntress of Nature? As a side note, it has often amazed me how many of my women friends have loved cats. I often wonder if their love for cats reflected a love for the power of their femininity. Furthermore, I wonder why terms such as *pussy* became associated with being inferior. I would never tell a lioness she was inferior. She might have me for lunch in enticing me to reflect on the devouring nature of the pussy.

To understand the historical evolution of how women became associated with the cat; we should begin with the ancient Egyptians. According to Walkers (1983), the Egyptian word for *cat* was *Mau.* This term served as an imitation of the cat's "Meow," and a mother syllable. The Greek historian named Plutarch reflected upon the sacredness of this animal by showing how Egyptians carved her on the sistrum of Isis as a metaphor for the Moon (Blair, 1993, p. 134). The linkage of cats to the Moon was because cats were nocturnal animals and great huntresses. Being nocturnal, the cat was metaphorically linked to the mysterious dark, the unknown.

The linkage of the cat to the Goddess is evident in the medieval belief that cats had nine lives. This belief continues metaphorically to this day. The association of the cat to the number nine unfolds from an ancient Egyptian representation of the *Ennead,* the *Nine Principles of Divinity* through the mythic image of the *Nine-Fold Cat Goddess* (Walkers, 1983).

Modern day cartoons and fairy tales often associate cats with witchcraft. In the not-too-distant past, Christians exposed cats to torture and fire along with witches. At medieval festivities, it was often customary to burn cats in wicker cages because they were linked with Satanism or evil. This type of torture and destruction of cats in Europe probably helped the spread of the plague. The decreases in the population of cats led to an increase in the rat population of Europe. "It's not nice to fool Mother Nature," the advertisement used to say. I wonder what kinds of horrors are going to manifest as a result of our disregard for the environment? It is likely that the recent influx of hurricanes and other extreme weather events is but a beginning of our seeing the results of our acts.

OF WITCHES AND CATS
During the middle ages, the majority of people tortured and murdered for being witches were women. Often, this

inexcusable abuse towards women was the result of sadism. These sadists used religious theology as an excuse to torture and rape women. In some cases, the destruction of a "witch" was the result of the actions of a physician who was threatened by her skills in healing.

The hatred and abuse of both women and cats emanate from their association with the ancient Goddess. People who were (and still are) witches engage in a Goddess-based Nature religion. In healing, their focus was and remains on natural mixtures, herbs and remedies. In Christian terminology, people who engage in Nature worship are *pagans*. In modern times, being called a pagan is a fate worse than death. The term links us to the ungodly, ignorant, evil and the atheistic. It has been a term that only finds its sacredness amongst motorcycle gangs and satanic worshippers. Only recently, have small groups of Americans begun to announce proudly their Pagan beliefs, often still to be hounded by the Christian majority.

Unfortunately, we live in ignorance of the original meaning of pagan. The term derives from the Latin *paganus*. It literally means *country dweller* (Walkers, 1983). In the name of what God have we burnt people at the stake; caused them to succumb to rape and torture; and damned them into hell for being country dwellers?! The perception of the pagans as evil unfolded from the resistance of Nature-oriented country peoples of medieval Europe to the anti-Nature and anti-female doctrines of a church that did not know its origins. Our attitude towards witches unfolds from a medieval political desire to control a population of people, mostly women. These people resisted a feudal religious and political doctrine that suppressed their way of life. That doctrine entailed and demanded the country dweller's (peasant's) slavery to the rich aristocratic leaders of a church. The teachings of this church went counter to the centuries-old way of living entailing freedom through the love and worship of the Great Mother.

CINDERELLA

Remnants of the peasants' resistance to the church unfold in the classic story of *Cinderella* (Walkers, 1983). The name of this heroine is a conjunction of *Cinder* and *Ella*. It refers to the ashes or cinders, of *Ella*, the Greek Fire-Goddess as *Hella* or *Helen*. The evil stepmother in this story is a metaphor for the church, according to Walkers (1983). The evil stepsisters serve as metaphors for the military aristocracy and clergy of the church. The Fairy Godmother in the story is the Goddess *Fate*. Interestingly, she turned the peasant into a Princess. Watch out all you rich aristocrats of modern times! No wonder Cinderella scares you!

When I sit and meditate on Cinderella's story, it sings to me. Stories such as this are not just made up fantasies. They are about us. What the exact meanings of the metaphors are makes no difference. Cinderella is enslaved as a peasant (in our days, laborers or the lower class) and realizes her richness via the Fairy Godmother, Sophia Herself. The ultimate goal of Cinderella's life is transcendence of her peasantry by Love. In my reading, Cinderella's story is the story of Psyche, the Soul. Her true love is Love himself, and it is to him that she is to be wed. This is not just a made up story. It is the work of Fate. It is true for each one of us.

In Christian theology, this Goddess became an evil. Most "idols" and graven images were statuary representations of the Goddess. In *The Red Tent*, Anita Diamant explores the transition from Goddess worship and honoring of the feminine to the Judeo-Christian-Muslim singular male God. A story early in this novel, expanding upon just a sentence in the Bible, tells how Rachel prevents Isaac from smashing their cherished goddess statues by sitting on a trunk containing them during her menstrual flow. He stormed away, unable to search the trunk, for it had become taboo for men to have anything to do with menstrual blood. The ancient ritual of blessing the earth with a girl's first flow persisted only covertly. So began the fall of women from cultural grace and power that persists to this day. *The Red Tent* explores this initial period of demonizing women in exquisite and gory detail.

This transformation manifests in the fear of burning in *Hell's* fires. The term *Hell* derives from the Greek Goddess, *Helle*. In Germany, *Hella* was *Hel* and it was through her that one found immortality (Walkers, 1983). Within Christianity this became known as purgatory in which we were purged of our sins in entering ecstatic union with God. In some cultures, she was under title of *Abundia or Satia*. These words serve as the ground for our modern day abundance and satiate. Overall, ancients did not consider the underworld a place of torment by an evil God (i.e., Satan). Rather, they viewed it as primarily dark, mysterious and awesome. At worst, it reflected general unhappiness of being dead (the Hellenistic Greek Hades). At best, it was Paradise.

One of the excuses given for the maltreatment of women in western culture is the story of Adam and Eve. In that story, God created the first woman out of the rib of a man named Adam. She eventually met up with a serpent that seduced her into eating an apple (the fruit that bore the knowledge of Good and Evil), which God had forbidden the primordial couple to eat. She then fed that apple to her husband. In conjunction with the words of the Bible, church officials said that the world has fallen into sin because of these naughty actions of Eve and the serpent. Due to this misconduct: Snakes slither on the ground; we are born in sin; women give birth in pain; and men have to toil in the fields because Adam listened to a woman. (Only very recently have we begun to see revisionist versions of this interpretation. A bumper sticker I saw recently, for instance, declared, "Yes, God created man before woman. Artists always make a rough draft before completing their masterpiece.")

According to the church, because of Eve's misbehavior and seduction of Adam to follow her, we have to repent (i.e., be saved), before we get to heaven. Being saved generally entails displacing our focus on our natural abilities to explore in the quest for the Spirit of Truth. We are to displace our natural powers and surrender to the external power of the church. We are to deny our natural hungers and desires as evil, thereby undermining our own dignity and power.

The church replaces the immanence of the Holy Spirit, dwelling immediately, *without any need of interpretation*, within all life. From day one of our lives, society teaches distrust of the Holy Spirit. For political reasons involving the control of the population, that distrust radiates from the church. Why else have great mystics like Meister Eckhart, Jacob Boehme and others have been excommunicated and slandered at best or executed at worse?

ADAM AND EVE

According to many current day scholars, the story of Adam and Eve unfolds from the desire of Hebrew priests to suppress Goddess worship. For example, the apple was one of her sacred fruits and served as a metaphor for Lady Wisdom. The linkage of the apple to Sophia becomes clear in cutting the fruit in cross-sections. The seeds are in the shape of a pentagram, the five-point star. Pythagorean mystics worshipped this star. They called it the *Pentalpha; the birth-letter (A) interlaced five times* (Graves, 1948). "A's" meaning was *Life or Health* and served as a metaphor for *Love*. The linkage of the apple to Sophia continues to this day through children who give their teachers apples as gifts. The apple is the fruit of knowledge. It was through the eating of this fruit that Adam and Eve saw themselves as naked. The apple opened their eyes. It made them self-aware. If there is any sin intended, it is that Adam and Eve became self-conscious. They became ashamed. Repentance from this sin should entail our attending church naked! Perhaps this would entice them to make easier seats than those cold, uniformly dreary benches focused on a talking head behind a pedestal that tells you he knows God's will.

Another interpretation that I personally like of the Adam and Eve story is that the eating of the apple was a metaphor for knowledge of farming which then caused us to labor in toil (i.e., to work hard for our living). The story of Cain and Abel further supports this interpretation, for Abel was a nomadic herdsman and was closer to the lifestyle of the tribal cultures that worked, on average, about four hours per day. Cain, in contrast, was an agriculturalist. Hence the story from this perspective reflected a historical movement. According to these interpretations, we should repent from sin by going naked and foraging in the wild! God will love us for it.

Similar to the apple and the cat, the serpent in the story of Adam and Eve symbolized the Goddess herself or her son and lover. The serpent was a perfect metaphor for the power that enticed Eve into eating the fruit of knowledge, for it was a general belief during ancient times that snakes do not die of old age. They periodically shed their skin and emerge renewed into another life (Walkers, 1983). In other words, snakes served as a metaphor for the birth-death-rebirth process.

In many cultures, the serpent was a metaphor for God as the son, lover and consort of the Goddess. He was the dying and resurrected God. Indeed, according to Walkers, the original Eve had no spouse, save the serpent, who was a living entity she created for her enjoyment. (Walkers, 1983) This version of Eve speaks to the *Euryonome*, the *Universal One*, who danced upon the primordial Ocean and created the serpent God, *Ophion* (Graves, 1948). This God became intoxicated by the dance of the Mother and curled himself about her luscious limbs to couple with her. Impregnated by this act, the Mother transformed herself into a dove (the modern day Holy Spirit) and laid the World Egg. Ophion eventually became arrogant and began calling himself the Creator. For this arrogance, Euryonome bruised his head with her heel and cast him into the underworld (probably her womb). This myth blatantly reflects the following lines of God to the serpent in Genesis: 3:15:

I shall put enmity between you and the woman,
and between your offspring and hers;
It will bruise your head
and you will strike its head.

At the time Genesis was written, matriarchal religions were still thriving. As stated, the serpent was a powerful metaphor relating to the Goddess. Perhaps the enmity between the serpent and the Woman was between women and their powers? In the case of serpent as lover, perhaps the enmity was between women and their enjoyment of sexuality? This notion manifested in the church, where beliefs were that women should not enjoy the sensual pleasures of sex. They should only enter the act to procreate the species.

Often this belief turned into an absurd and inexcusable evil against women and girls. For example, in recent times, doctors use to identify girls who developed orgasmic capabilities through masturbation as medical problems. In the

United States, the latest cure for this sickness occurred in 1948, when a 5-year-old girl had her clitoris removed by surgery because of her self-exploration (Walkers, 1983). The inhumane practice of clitoris removal is still practiced in some Muslim cultures. Likewise, the sadistic practice of vaginal sewing, which occurs in this culture to ensure a girl's chastity until the day of her wedding is still common procedures for doctors in the Middle East. On her wedding night, the man tears the threads open with a knife. The next day, he proudly displays the bloodstained knife to his friends.

It should be noted that *clitoris* derives from the Greek *kleitoris,* meaning *divine, famous or Goddess-like* (Walkers, 1983). The wounding of a woman's body is the desecration of what is sacred to God.

The dominant patriarchal interpretation of Eve is far from the only way to tell her story. Some of the other ways, discarded as heresy by a distinctly patriarchal and misogynistic Church, allow us another analysis of this allegory for the human condition. It is no secret that Gnostic Christians identified Eve with Zoë or Life. In this tradition, Eve is seen as the animating principle of Adam. Interestingly, the path of the Feminine or Goddess is the left-hand path. This is the path of the heart, of compassion, for the heart leans to the left. Hence, one of Sophia's names is "Understanding". Understanding is comprehension and comprehension is compassion for it entails a bonding. If you say to someone, "I understand," this means you comprehend her and are bonding yourself to her. The same bonding happens with an idea. When you understand an idea, you comprehend it and integrate or bond it into yourself.

In modern days, this left-right dichotomy acts itself out in our political battles where the so-called *left-wing* are seen as *bleeding heart liberals* with more feminine values of providing for people (e.g., social services, understanding, compassion) than the so-called *right-wing* with its more masculine focus on dominance and control both internally (e.g., abortion, law and order) and externally (e.g., domination of world oil markets through militarization and war). It appears this pitting of left and right is an ancient struggle for humanity. When shall we hold hands and marry this basic divisional mindset?

The point to all this is that everything contains everything else. The universe is a web spun by Sophia in such a way that every point mirrors all other points. In India, this translates as the Heaven of the Goddess Indra; which contains an infinite number of jewels that mirror and contain all other jewels. The Bible is no different. Beneath the seemingly linear movement across time, themes manifest in a nonlinear fashion and continually change their face. The image of New Jerusalem's descent to Her Bridegroom in Revelations is the image of Joshua's marriage to Rehab. Rehab is Tehom as the primordial Waters of Genesis: 1:2. The Womb and Tomb of Creation are not two. Furthermore, the marriage of Christ at the end of Revelations mirrors the marriage of the Sun God in various mythologies across the world. This means this is *not* an isolated book written by Hebrews 3,000 years ago. **In its depths, the Bible reaches its arms out and embraces the entire world in its arms**. This is the beauty of it.

In the next chapter, we will move beyond history into the here and now. We will take a deeper look at what fears keep us from truly loving the Feminine by taking a look at how she scares the shit out of us. Why else would she be so abused and suppressed? Only fear creates that kind of behavior.

Chapter 12
The Lovely Web She Weaves
⌒⌒

Oh, what a lovely web she weaves
When first she ventures to conceive
~ My revision of Sir Walter Scott

In order to create harmony on Earth, an initial, crucial step must be to transform our current system of thought. Our seldom questioned belief in a dualistic, warring universe, with scarce resources over which one must maintain control, has gotten us into a systemic mess of environmental degradation, economic collapse, and factional warring. This mindset of scarcity and a resultant need for domination is mirrored by our international, interpersonal and intrapersonal conflicts. Our way out of these conflicts is a realization of a universe grounded in infinite potential. This transformative thought will set us free to find our natural home in the loving arms of peace. We will find ourselves securely held within the lovely web Sophia weaves. We will realize we are all prodigal children whom the Holy Spirit has called home, right where we belong in the lap of Love, and–like Dorothy upon her return to Kansas from Oz–right where we have unwittingly been right along.

"Blessed are the peacemakers," says the Beloved (Matthew 5:9). This same Beloved further chastises his disciples, who don't believe they can weather the upcoming storm, for having "little faith." (Matthew 8:25). Just as Jesus calmed their stormy sea, we need to calm our stormy relationships. Belief (indeed, knowledge) is paramount to change. If we know and manifest peace, trust peace, and live peace, then peace will unfold. If we believe peace, trust peace, and live peace, then peace will unfold. How do we develop such faith in the face of the crises we face politically, economically, personally, and ecologically? This transformation will require a major paradigm shift from one of scarcity–which necessitates fear, greed, and violence–to one of abundance--which invites hope, charity, and peacefulness.

In this chapter, I will explore how we can facilitate such a paradigm shift. We must hasten this transformation of our cultural mindset, for the hour is late if we are to avoid what appears to be inevitable catastrophe. Fortunately, such a paradigm shift is already underway among many of the leading thinkers in the fields of eco-psychology, physics, life sciences, anthropology, mythology, philosophy, deep ecology, and eco-feminism. Thought in these purportedly diverse fields is converging upon a paradigm of abundance and potential. I wish to highlight and celebrate this convergence, which I believe to be humankind's greatest hope for continuing evolution for our species and all the related species upon our planet.

Our Mother Earth is already showing signs of simply succumbing to the death of the current generation of life forms and starting anew. In huge "dead spots" within the ocean, a form of toxic algae has re-emerged which has been considered extinct since the emergence of life eons ago. (Solow, 2004) If we do not wish to go the way of the dinosaurs, taking with us all that we know and love in the biosphere, we need to co-operate in healing our Mother STAT! How do we do so?

PARADIGM SHIFT TO A PARTNERSHIP MODEL

The first stage in coming into peace and sustainability is to understand the belief system that we are spreading world-wide. This meme is shaping our perceptions and behavior. Eisner (1988) identifies two primary ways of relating throughout history: the domination model and the partnership model. These models are used to describe all relationships, be they between humanity and Nature, man and woman, nation and nation, one religion and another, or warring parts within ourselves. In order to cross over from the domination model, current in so much western and globalized modern culture, to the partnership model, common to most ancient and indigenous cultures, we would have to see these relationships as complementary rather than adversarial. We need to redevelop the partnership mindset in our relations to each other and to our Earth.

David Bohm (2002) reveals why the partnership model is much more realistic, fitting the nature of all things in the universe more truly than does the dominating model. Bohm states the universe is akin to a holographic image where each part mirrors and contains the whole. A functional understanding of this principle may be behind the miracle Jesus works when he feeds the multitude from seven loaves and fishes (Matthew 15: 34-36). This idea is beautifully imaged in Deepak Chopra's (1993) *Ageless Body, Timeless Mind* where the reader is led on a guided journey into the interior world beneath her surface skin (p. 42). As the reader proceeds through the journey, she soon finds the atoms in her body are contained in emptiness as vast as intergalactic space. Going even further, she soon finds herself with depths and potentialities that extend into infinity.

Bohm claims that an "Unmanifest Implicate Order" provides the foundation of the holographic universe. I interpret his unmanifest as the same dark, internal no-thingness, this infinity of potentials at which we arrive in the Chopra meditation. This unmanifest is also what we encounter in the empty spaces within any object we examine under an extremely powerful microscope. In this place of no-thingness, there are an infinite number of possibilities that float about us like unfertilized eggs that could manifest at the correct seminal moment. I further relate the unmanifest to the dark chaotic ocean and night Goddesses of the past, such as the Sumerian Tiamat, Etruscan Nix, Indian Kali, Kogis Aluna, Keres Pueblo Thinking Woman, Hebrew Tehom and the Kabbalist Ain Soph. Indeed, I would venture to say this unmanifest is our Soul, who remains the essence of our being, at one with the universe, eternally beyond the time-space loop of birth and death, yet holding within Her womb all our potentials yet to unfold. We cannot locate our Soul within our manifest body, yet we are intuitively and spiritually aware that she is the queen of our being, more deeply *true* than the palpable facts of our life.

Manifestation is the unfolding of one among the multitude of potentials within our Soul, which is called forth and stirred to life by a seminal occurrence. Partnership societies are one of a multitude of possibilities manifesting along with those that are domineering. Hence, we can unfold a peaceful society.

As discussed in chapter 6, the holographic universe theory of each part mirroring the whole encompasses all our cognitions, such as thoughts, beliefs and perceptions, which are systemic reflections of our cultural beliefs (Bohm, 1994). As we think and believe, so we act, and so we are acted upon. We reap what we sow. Moreover, we save the seed to sow again next spring and reap again next autumn in an ongoing cycle.

BEYOND WAR
A belief in scarcity, including its resultant need for dominance and control, necessitates war, empire, slave labor, mass agribusiness, hoarding, and abuse. These cognitions have evolved as part of the dominating mindset over the past four or five thousand years with the advent of civilization and our "divorce" from Nature.

Indeed, our deep, culturally shared belief in and fear of scarcity may be responsible for much of the scarcity we actually experience. Our belief system is almost certainly seminal in what we manifest individually as poverty and globally as starvation and resource depletion. We are looking, here, at the deeper principle underlying what we call "self-fulfilling prophecy." Fear breeds terrorism. (Indeed, fear of terrorism breeds faster than bunnies, producing a rash of terrorists among both the feared and the fearful. Witness today's "war on terror"!) Once we believe in something deeply and clearly enough to fear it, we inseminate the potential monster we fear, bringing it to manifestation. *"And the beat goes on."* We fail to see that we are trapped in a web of our own making. When we hear of an alternative while trapped within our paradigm, it is likely to appear far-fetched. We may dismiss it as unrealistic or naïve, because it does not see reality from our perspective.

Consider the proposal for a Department of Peace to balance the Department of War, recently renamed the Department of Defense to feed into our fears of vulnerability in a world of scarcity. Rather than working from this perspective of terror and competition for scarce resources, Congressman Dennis Kucinich's *Department of Peace* proposal arises from a different relational, integrative perspective. While not formally named as such, Eisner's dream of returning to a partnership model is the impetus underlying the proposed *Department of Peace.* It only sounds far-fetched and unrealistic to those still blind to an alternative paradigm to dominance.

This proposal couldn't get off the ground with the current dualistic and fear-driven mindset of congress and our culture. Developing such a department and unfolding a true partnership society upon this Earth must entail acknowledging, confronting, and transforming our current mindset of dualism, individualism and antagonism that discounts and minimizes relational thought.

Now, however, times may be changing. David Swanson, author of *War No More: The Case for Abolition,* has a website at www.worldbeyondwar.org where people can sign on to the following pledge:

> *I understand that wars and militarism make us less safe rather than protect us, that they kill, injure and traumatize adults, children and infants, severely damage the natural environment, erode civil liberties, and drain our economies, siphoning resources from life-affirming activities. I commit to engage in and support nonviolent efforts to end all war and preparations for war and to create a sustainable and just peace.*

Not only are people flocking to the website to sign, but many are asking, "How can I contribute money? How can I help?" even before the site is fully functional.

Only when we develop faith that we are holographic images of an all-providing, life-supporting universe, will we trust our God. Only then will we trust ourselves, our brothers and sisters, and our Earth to sustain us in peace and prosperity. We cannot "consider the lilies of the field" as relevant to our condition unless we believe them to be our sisters, another holographic image of the same source from which we arise. Clearly, a paradigmatic transformation is a crucial forerunner of such a radical political change as a Department of Peace. Just the discussion of the possibility helps to foster this paradigmatic leap.

In dualistic thought, there is a basic separation of the person from all others and the environment as a whole. Indeed, there are even basic intrapersonal divisions between the unconscious and the conscious minds and between body, mind, and spirit in such a mindset. In contrast, relational thinking is evidenced in tribal cultures that see the unity of body-mind-spirit, acknowledge Nature as our primal Mother, embed the individual in the tribe, look to the ancestors for guidance, and consider the effects of their choices on their progeny unto the seventh generation. In other words, relational thinking is characterized by understanding how the individual relates to all events, things, and people past, present, and future. For example, if one were to build a chemical plant and were thinking relationally, one would take a look the environmental impact on other people, other places within the ecosystem, and other times. There would be much more taken into account than the "bottom line". In holistic thinking, the bottom line is only one of the many lines that weave throughout a multidimensional system and, moreover, tie it to the rest of the universe.

In the paradigm shift integrating spirituality, philosophy, and science occurring today (Capra, 1999) there is a return to this more ancient relational way of understanding the universe. Interestingly, the term *revolution* means to come full circle. What is *revolutionary*, meaning breaking anew from the status quo, paradoxically proves also to be *revolutionary*, meaning cyclically returning to its beginnings. Hence, we seem to be returning to what we once knew through the language of myth and metaphor. Indeed, in the relational view of the new paradigm, there is a rekindled respect for metaphor. As Bateson (2000) states, metaphor is Nature's language and is the language that connects. Hence, the male and female bodies can be seen as metaphors that reflect processes that are eminent throughout the universe. In this kind of realization, alienation will fall by the wayside.

Katzenback (2005) reflects upon the dire warnings about the dangers of divisive solar, masculine, individualistic thinking that are revealed in Sophocles' play, *Oedipus Rex*. Sophocles writes that a son is born to King Laius and Queen Jocasta of Thebes. After Laius learns from an oracle that "he is doomed/To perish by the hand of his own son", he orders Jocasta to kill the infant. Hesitant to do so, she orders a servant to commit the act for her. Instead, the servant gives the baby to a shepherd who names him Oedipus. The shepherd carries the baby with him to Corinth, where Oedipus is taken in and raised in the court of the childless King Polybus of Corinth as if he were his own. Yet another child is hidden from a murderous, jealous king whose status quo is threatened!

Katzenback shows how this paradigm, which Sophocles already recognized as catastrophic millennia ago, relates to our ecological mess. In looking at *Oedipus Rex* in conjunction with *Oedipus at Colonus,* the author points out that Sophocles is reflecting upon the journey of Oedipus as being the transformation of the Soul for the sake of the Earth. It is this transformation of the Soul that we will focus on in this chapter. Moreover, we will focus on how the Soul can transform us!

As is true with all mythology, the hero's task is our own (Campbell, 1968). This unity of story and personal history supports Bohm's notion of the holographic universe for the myths are *our* stories. The hero of mythology is not some made up character fantasized by people without the great insights into the universe we supposedly have in our modern age of reductionist science. Oedipus is not different from us as a tragic hero. As Freud realized, through his theory of the Oedipal Complex, his story is ours. Unfortunately, Freud didn't realize the full ramifications of the story, nor did he relate it to how we have blinded ourselves to the rape of Nature, which, ultimately, is our own rape. What we do to others, we do to ourselves (Katzenback, 2005).

If we are to face up to our modern relationship to the Earth as an incestuous rape, we must begin by understanding the term *nature* as meaning *essence*. Nature is our Soul, writ large. Nature is the essence of who we are, our true being. We dimly acknowledge this relationship when we speak of "human nature." If we acknowledge that we are integral to Nature and she is integral to us, it becomes our most pressing task to allow the Soul to transform us to engage in a more connective relationship with the Earth. In that connection, we will begin to see our soul and the soul of the Earth as united in harmonious Love. Hence, the singular commandment, the Golden Rule, "Love thy neighbor as thyself," will become our operational mindset. Indeed, in realizing our infinity, we will understand that no two things exist side-by-side. That which appears separate is but a different holographic image of the whole. Our neighbor *is* our self and how we treat him determines how we are treated in turn.

Both women and nature are seen in globalized culture and many contemporary religions, including Judaism, Islam and Christianity, as fallen, inferior creatures. I believe that much of this attacking of the feminine reveals a fear of the Deep Feminine, the wild psyche that swallows and disintegrates, that lies unconsciously in both male and female minds. Indeed, going into this place could spell a loss of control and hence a death of sorts. Yet, as the metaphor of going into a cave reveals, it is there in those Feminine depths that we find our deepest treasure.

Osho (2005) states the Feminine is the agent of all change, of evolution. Only in the indefinite, unfilled, feminine, internal space within them do the walls constructed by the masculine external labor become a room or a home. Without her unmanifest no-thingness, the universe collapses back upon itself and ceases to have life. All potential for new creation, evolution, or healing dwells in the feminine Unmanifest.

Furthermore, the anatomy of the human female reflects this evolutionary role that the Feminine has in the universe. Indeed, a woman's body is a major and dramatic change from the bodies of the rest of the female animals with whom we share this planet. Unlike other female animals, the human woman is able to engage in intercourse at any time and is not tied to times of heat during which she is most likely to become impregnated. Furthermore, her genitals are positioned more to the front, which allows for intercourse face-to-face. The primary effect of these changes is to allow greater intimacy and love. It would seem from this development in the bodies of women that our evolutionary purpose is to love.

DESIGNED FOR LOVE
We must embrace this realization: **We are designed to love!** The human body makes us almost ridiculously vulnerable. Our upright stance exposes organs that are protected under the frame of other mammals. Our lack of fur further exposes us to heat and cold (which may be part of the reason we began to interpret the natural elements as our enemy). The size of our brain requires an abnormally long,

slow developmental period when we are entirely dependent on our parents. This same brain has come up with ingenious weapons with which to kill or torture one another. Come to think of it: it is no wonder that we developed a mindset of fear and scarcity. Only Love, fostered in the atmosphere of faith, hope, and compassion propounded by all our great spiritual teachers, can protect us.

How, then, are we living up to our purpose to love? Isn't such lived-out love what Jesus tried to impart in his teachings? Isn't the living out of the imperative to love what the new paradigm of a relational universe is trying to impart? Such Love–whether expressed in interpersonal one-on-one relationships, through intrapersonal self-worth, between human and God, between creature and Earth, or among tribes–is made possible by the feminine principle within the Universe.

This is important to realize, for if we are locked into patriarchy's masculine dominance model of being a controlling power, be it corporate, governmental, or religious, then the feminine is a threat. This threat is the death of the status quo, for the feminine impulse brings forth a change that means our transformation or death through the birth of a new paradigm. This transforming power of the Feminine is reflected outright in the Bible's "Book of Hagia Sophia," alternatively titled "The Wisdom of Solomon," where Sophia is described as unchanging yet renewing the world. Solomon understood that Sophia dwelt at his very heart, as his very own Soul.

The first way we can express the Love much needed to heal our divisiveness is to resist misogyny wherever we experience it, whether towards individual women, womankind, the feminine impulses within men, Mother Earth, or the worship of the Goddess. In the words of a Tantric scripture, we must:

Look upon every woman as a Goddess,
whose special energy she is,
and honor her in that state.

—*Uttara Tantra* (Austin, 1990, 126)

If we are grounded in our feminine power, then we have at our disposal a plentitude of power. However, by becoming blinded by the sun, i.e., our surface consciousness, we have become deluded into believing that we live in a world of scarce resources. The surface solar consciousness, enshrined by our patriarchal, misogynistic cultural mindset, creates poverty for the rich as much as the poor because the rich man thinks he lives in a limited world and has to hoard the scarce resources by whatever means possible, even killing. Yet, his mind is as impoverished as the poor man. Indeed, the poor man might be richer by realizing the universe is unlimited. I have seen many a struggling artist who continues his art because his love for what he does is unlimited. He sees his wealth in his art, which is infinite in its variability. To understand this idea metaphorically, consider how far you can see looking up into the sunlit daytime skies and how much farther you can see on a clear night. Why, in the supposed "dark" of a clear night, you can see light years away into events that happened thousands of years ago!!

As Bohm's theory of the holographic universe would predict, myths play themselves out throughout each one of us. The part mirrors the whole. In my opinion, the myths live themselves out in the way we approach our so-called Unconscious, which again is filled with infinite potential. My thesis here is that the individualized consciousness is scared of not being in control and hence is scared of his death. For a moment, pause and think about what such a reality would mean politically as well as psychologically.

This fear of the loss of power is the heart of the fear of the Goddess and true Creativity. It is the suppression of Nature, which means more than birds, bees and coconut trees. It means our Essence or Truth. Do you think the powers-that-be truly want you to be you or what they want you to be? Authentic people, true to themselves, such as Jesus, Martin Luther King, or Mahatma Gandhi are an intolerable threat to authority and are murdered.

OF KING HEROD AND KING CULTURE

Goethe (1959) wrote in *Faust*, "*The eternal Feminine draws us onward*." In this line, he is again realizing the Feminine as the agent of change. If we think of Mary as the Soul or the divine Ocean who gives birth to a new level of consciousness, then suppression is needed by the powers-that-be to keep her powers in check. After all, evolution means death to the ruling King (our cultural paradigm). He does not want to surrender the scarce resources that he desperately hoards. He frantically defends the status quo against all revolution or evolution. Yet, this tyrant has no sense of the consequences of his acts. He does not see his own enslavement to the goods and resources he believes enhance his status and security. This is why Jesus says, "Forgive them Father for they do not know what they are doing." King Culture, like King Laius, father of Oedipus, is caught up in his limited world and can't hear the evolutionary message. He does not know that we can walk on water, heal the sick, and heal the planet.

Because King Herod was fearful of being overthrown, Mary and Joseph had to take the Child Jesus into hiding in Egypt. King Culture is likewise fearful of being overthrown. (Consider, for instance, the Koch brothers, oil and coal barons, whose monumental profits are threatened by renewable energy sources.) The King, the individualized consciousness, locked into his ruling class, is fearful of his demise and hence sets out to destroy the Divine Child, the new consciousness that mirrors the old and takes it to a new level. The need for us to hide this Divine Child within ourselves is not peculiar to Christian mythology. It is evident throughout the world. The story of Moses being sent off in a basket to be raised by Pharaoh's wife only to lead his people out of slavery is an example of this repeating story. This same drama manifests through Zeus who is hidden by his Mother Rhea to keep him from being eaten by his Father, Saturn. The story of Oedipus, hidden from Laius, fits this pattern. In the movie, *Willow*, Aluna must be hidden and protected from the witch, fearful of losing her power; and in *Snow White*, the dwarves hide the princess from her jealous stepmother. These stories reveal the same theme: the Divine Child, the child of the evolutionary Soul, is a threat and must be taken into hiding.

This process is mirrored in the individual, externally oriented male consciousness that is afraid of letting go to the inner feminine that is his wilderness within. Instead, he holds onto his power manifested externally. In other words, he sees his power as being through the control of others, acquiring political power, accumulating wealth, or being intellectual. In psychological terms, our conscious mind is afraid of letting go to the hidden depths, the source of our true treasures, the so-called unconscious that is more conscious than what is called the conscious.

Jesus calls himself the *Son of Man* because he is the manifestation of evolutionary consciousness that each one of us carries within as potential. We hide him away for fear of danger from the powers that be, including our own belief system! He is indeed *our* son, for it is our virgin Soul that births him, and it is she that hides him. There is a woman with twelve stars over her head in Revelations that has to

168

hide her child from the avenging monster. Do you recognize her? She is you hiding your Truth!

THE RETURN OF THE DIVINE CHILD

Yet, this Divine Child is already reborn and walks among us. He is not a literal child, but a holistic movement given birth by our Soul. He is still small and not yet well known by the status quo. He is still newly born, though he is ancient. He needs nurturing and love to grow. He grows in the wombs that are marrying spirituality and science. He walks in the new science that sees Gaia, the Earth, as a living being. He thrives in the recognition of the universe as an interrelated web. He plays with those who are true lovers of Peace. Yet he continues to hide from those who speak peace while pitting themselves up against a perceived enemy to conserve what they interpret to be the source of their wealth and power.

The Divine Child is indeed the Child of Mary, when she is recognized as the divine feminine power of marriage or union. As the child of Heaven and Earth, he conjoins all opposites in honor of his Mother. He resolves the central paradox of diversity within unity by revealing all opposites and adversaries to be complements and mirror images of each other. He embodies the Trinity, revealing the transcendent God, the human manifestation, and the invisible but invincible Soul within to be One, the universal principle. He walks among us in many forms awaiting his bride, Jerusalem. He reveals her to be our universal Place of Peace, not just some war-savaged city in the Middle East.

Indeed, he walks with me in the stillness of my heart, for it is there, in the stillness between beats, that he is indeed living in Peace. Our Lord is ancient, yet he is born anew in our hearts, our Eva-Maria. Though he is revolutionary, in the sense that he comes full circle to complete the Wisdom

169

of the ancients; he is also revolutionary, in the alternative sense that he is the flower of the newly evolving humanity, never looking the same or as we expect from prior manifestations. He is the Son of Infinity-Eternity wedded, by Love, to earthly space-time. He is God welcoming home the prodigal child, humanity, as a beloved member of the divine family.

To summarize, I would maintain that we appear stuck in pollution, war, economic collapse, petroleum dependence, and our individualized psychological sicknesses, because we are stuck in our attachment to our current system of thought. That system of thought is reflected in the drama of Oedipus and the story of Adam and Eve, wherein an isolated or individualized ego is born. This consciousness sees the world as limited, having scarce resources that need to be protected through any means possible, including murder, war, and the suppression of various people. In this vision of scarcity, we bio-engineer ever new monocropped food sources, blind to how we are destroying Nature's soil, water, air, and bio-diversity that are the true and eternal source of food.

The way to peace and ecological wellbeing upon the planet is to bring forth a newly born ancient consciousness of Love or Relatedness. We can call it Christ Consciousness. We can call it Buddha Consciousness. We can call it Krishna Consciousness. We can call it eco-consciousness. We can call it anything we want, for all are parts of one holographic universe. The Christ, the Buddha, Krishna and Gaia all mirror one another at a very deep level, as do their Mothers.

To bring this Consciousness forth, we have to understand what it is we need to change. I so want to deem as the enemy this consciousness in which we are historically embedded. Yet, such an adversarial, hateful interpretation of our relationship to those who think differently from us will hinder the development and birth of the new Consciousness. To call the old consciousness an enemy is to pit one consciousness against the other. "Make love, not war!" the hippies cry. There is much wisdom in this.

Dueling paradigms will not advance our cause! Rather we must seek out, inseminate, and nurture the seed of yin that lies at the heart of yang, always realizing that we are complements, not adversaries, of those who hold onto the patriarchal paradigm. We need only to look into the fear of looming extinction or planetary destruction that sometimes grips our own hearts to have compassion for the fear in the hearts of the patriarchs. Fear is fear, whatever mask it wears. The only remedy is the faith that Love makes possible.

We are all in this fragile Earthship together. Nobody gets thrown overboard or left to freeze in the cold sea without bringing death and destruction to the "survivors." Just ask the ancient mariner who had to learn to embrace with love the albatross hung about his neck by a vengeful crew! Only when he could see the beauty in the loathsome bird and forgive his crew was he freed to return to land, required to tell his (universal) story to all who would listen. We must believe that the Earth that birthed Martin Luther King, Jr. is also the Mother of the Koch brothers. Hidden within their hearts is the seed of mother-love, masked by their terror of surrender to the inner feminine. All saber flashing hides terrified little boys who can only be redeemed by Love.

The issue, then, is our dualistic thinking. Diabalos, the divider, strikes again! When we take a look at how we are relating to the world in this day and age, we are definitely in the clutches of a divisive consciousness. Today, we have the battle of male against female, left against right, children against parents against children, red state against blue state, and humanity against Nature. Internally this adversarial mindset creates war within ourselves, for we pit our conscious against our unconscious mind. We pit our appetites against our piety, our giving against our receiving, and our security against our compassion. Hence, control and domination rule the planet.

Yet, when we begin to see the world through holistic eyes, everyone and everything reappear as brothers and sisters. We realize and therefore make real, the unity of all things, from the tiniest speck of dust to the greatest mountain. In that realization of our relatedness, we will be able to bring peace to the planet, which, in turn, means peace to ourselves. It is then that we will find ourselves revealed or evolved as the Bridegroom, the one groomed for the bride—Peace, Love and Truth—herself. When that evolutionary, revolutionary change happens, the Gods will laugh, for the great joke will be revealed. We were inextricably married to her all along!

Chapter 13
Awakening to Wholeness
◇~◯

Is not Hochmah (Wisdom) calling?
Is not Binah (Understanding) raising her voice?
On the heights overlooking the road,
at the crossways, she takes her stand;
by the gates, at the entrance to the city,
on the access roads, she cries out:
"I am calling to you, all people,
my words are addressed to all humanity."
~ Proverbs: 8:14

In the summer months of 1993, I was working at a residential facility in Annapolis, Maryland, designed to help people diagnosed with a mental illness stay in the community. At times, I would work a crisis program within that facility that required me to serve some overnight shifts. One morning, I was driving home after one of these shifts when my thoughts drifted into a meditation on the Mahayana Bodhisattva Avalokiteshvara. It is interesting in the light of God as the Buddhists name him, that *Mahayana* means *Universal*, as does the term *Catholic*. May we come to truly embrace the Universal One. May we grow to accept that "One God" is an inclusive (everybody!) not an exclusive (only my sect!) understanding of the Divine Being. According to Buddhist thought, a Bodhisattva is a being that has forsaken bliss (nirvana) until all beings are prepared to enter into bliss before him. His compassion is towards all beings; be they ant, bird or human. He will appear to a spider as a spider, to a merchant as a merchant, and to a plant as a plant.

All beings can achieve such compassion. Quan Yin, She-Who-Hears-the-Cries-of-the-World, is such a Bodhisattva. The story goes that she gained compassion for all beings by nursing her father, although he had much abused her, even burning down the convent where she had retreated when she refused to marry as he had dictated, killing many of her Sisters. Because Kuan Yin's compassion became so great that she postponed Nirvana to hear and help all others find their way to bliss, she is now revered as a Goddess worldwide. I have seen her statue in many American homes. Such compassion is a more-than-human trait. There are many stories of dogs showing such compassion, including the one in *Marley and Me* of the dog grieving with the author's wife when she miscarried. (Grogan, 2006)

VISION: ONE SOUL

While contemplating Mahayana Bodhisattva Avalokiteshvara, I arrived at a stoplight and my attention suddenly shifted again. A vision arose before my eyes:

I saw a range of people. There were Orientals, Americans, Europeans, and Africans. I saw that even though they differed; they were one. All beings lived within an infinite Ocean of Consciousness. I realized that no matter what culture one belonged to, there was one Soul. In this state, I could see Sophia's transparency. Yet, I could not see her visually. All peoples were within her; she was apparent within all peoples. Everything existed as images arising within and dissolving back into the infinity of pure awareness.

All separations disappeared into oblivion. What was many became one. The entire universe revealed itself as Sophia. Everything I saw, everything I heard, and everything I smelt was She. I felt the sweetness of her breath descending from the heavens above me. I felt a spark, like a burning kiss of fire, radiate from the inner depths of my being. Every cell in my body erupted into fiery ecstasy at the touch of her lips. My cells were like blossoming flowers responding to the warmth of the Sun's rays. In response to her warmth and sweetness, my entire body appeared to radiate with energy of infinite magnitude. I became a burning fire of Love, ready to burst forth from the power surge encompassing me.

Sophia had just devoured me, for all distinctions between us disappeared. I was in a place where there were no categories, names, or definitions. I was in a place beyond thought, beyond the arising of the Word. Only the incomprehensible and infinite depths of my Mother remained. I had dissolved into Sophia's womb as the blackness of the eternal light. I was the Alpha and the Omega.

Ideas about God being within or without ceased to make sense. Immanence and transcendence were one and the same. There was no up, down, or sideways. The idea of size dissolved into obscurity. It appeared I was everywhere; yet, I was nowhere. In being no-where, I was now-here. I simultaneously was and was no longer. Only Sophia remained as I dissolved into my natural state of oceanic bliss. I had died and been reborn. I realized myself as the Son of Sophia. More than that, I realized I was Sophia for she was my very Nature.

Hence, in this vision I received my sacred name, Bensophia or Sophia's son.

The reader will probably recall I shared this sacred name with the boy whose story I told in chapter 9. His story of discovering his true adult identity as his mother's son is a metaphor for my story, as is all allegory. I joyfully share my name with him, as with all creation. It is uniquely mine and, simultaneously universal. Such is the paradox of Sophia's creation.

Isis describes herself to Lucius as "manifesting alone, under one form, all the Goddesses and Gods" (Apuleius, 1992, p. 264). When Isis spoke to Lucius, she was speaking to me. In my transcendent moment/eternity, I could see that there were no separate Gods of Christianity, Judaism, Muslim, Hindu, Buddhist, African, or Native American. When God said his name is simply "I-Am," he meant it! The Lord your God (his God; her God; all God) is *One* God, indivisible, however we individually name her. Distinctive male or female pronouns become irrelevant in the realm of the divine. They are necessary only in the limited language and vision of dualism. God and Goddess, like yin and yang, are one Being. This diversity-within-unity is the central and miraculous Mystery of Love. This is what the vision taught me. All Gods and Goddesses were expressions of Sophia. Conversely, "Sophia" is my personal way of addressing the one who encompasses all Gods and Goddesses. Furthermore, there was no separation between our Mother and us. Humanity, in its true essence, is not distinct or alienated from Deity, but rather an expression of his/her Nature (Essence). In their book, *The Myth of the Goddess: Evolution of an Image*, Baring and Cashford (1991, p. 353) beautifully describe our unity in the Mother, under the name of Aphrodite, below:

Consequently, she is the figure who, in the likeness of the original Goddess, brings back together the separate forms of her creation. In this sense, Aphrodite is 'born' when people joyfully remember, as a distinct and sacred reality, the bonds that exist between human beings and animals and, indeed, the whole of Nature. Myth proposes this happens through Love. Union is then reunion, for Love that begets life resounds with the mystery of life itself.

Baring and Cashford do an excellent job at linking ancient European and Middle Eastern Goddesses. They do this by revealing a universal theme behind the Mother-and-Child myths. Through reading this book, the lover of Sophia is able to obtain an in-depth knowledge of the Mother's powers to weave herself into the minds of women and men through various images, names, and ideas. On the surface, the Goddess appears to us as many. Yet, upon close scrutiny, her diversity is a hidden unity. Baring and Cashford summarize the unifying thread behind the various ideas of the Goddess and her Consort and Son, through their identification of the Greek ideas of *Zoë* and *Bios*. Here are their definitions of these beings:

Zoë is eternal and infinite life; Bios is finite and individual life. Zoë is Infinite Being; Bios is the living and dying manifestation of this eternal world in time. The Classical scholar Carl Kerenyi explains: 'Zoë is the thread upon which every individual Bios is strung like a bead and which, in contrast to Bios, can be conceived of only as endless – as infinite life.

(Baring & Cashford, p. 148)

If you understand this statement, you can understand all religions. Indeed, if you understand this statement, you understand everything. This idea of Zoë and Bios blatantly mirrors David Bohm's idea of the Unmanifest as being an infinite ocean of energy or life. It is this Ocean that serves as the ground for the surface world (the manifest) in which we live. The Unmanifest Implicate Order is nothing more than a fancy name for Zoë (Life). The Manifest Explicit Order is nothing more than a fancy name for Bios. Interestingly, in recently revealed Gnostic Christian and Jewish writings, Zoë is equated to life.

UNITY OF SCIENCE, MYTH, AND RELIGION

As many scientists are now beginning to rediscover, the universe is an integrated wholeness. This is not a new idea. It has been reborn after being buried in the deep recesses of our minds. Ancients professed this idea long before holistic science. In modern day research, physics has shown that a person's perception of his separateness from the world and other human beings is an illusion. Considering the basic unity behind Bohm's theory of the Unmanifest and the Greek idea of Zoë as Infinite Life, I would also maintain that science herself is not separate from ancient spirituality. Quantum Physics is nothing more than the old Mother and Child myths redressed in a new form.

For example, physicist Niels Bohr expresses the illusion of separateness by stressing quantum theory's revelation of the basic indivisibility (called virginity in ancient cosmology) of Nature (Peat, 1987, p. 74). Meanwhile, Heisenberg's *Uncertainty Principle* has indicated the extent to which a scientific observer intervenes in the systems he or she, observes. There is no such thing as a detached scientist observing the behavior of the universe in an objective fashion. Indeed, when Truth reveals herself, there is no distinction between the observing scientist and the observed phenomena. Subject and object are not two except in scientific dogma. Furthermore, the research scientist involves herself in creating the results she observes. This position indicates that scientists specifically, and human beings in general, cannot separate themselves from the world.

Contemplator Ken Wilber (1993) states that our "fall" is into dualism. His statement mirrors the beginning of Genesis where every time God speaks; the primordial waters divide. Indeed, according to Wilber, the arising of thought is ignorance in that thought generates the illusion of dualism. This has been the message of mystics throughout the ages within all cultures. Coming into grace is not about praying for and receiving a new car. It is about smashing the illusion of separateness. This is the condition before the fall into duality. This is Eden.

The idea of our basic indivisibility from Nature receives its most potent expression through the Mother-and-Child myths. The way we relate to a human woman as a child mirrors and equals how we relate to Nature. Philosopher Norman O. Brown (1959, p. 52) expresses this idea:

> *At the mother's breast, in Freudian language, the child experiences that primal condition, forever after idealized, "in which object-libido and ego-libido cannot be distinguished;" in philosophical language, the subject-object dualism does not corrupt the blissful experience of the child at the mother's breast. The primal childhood experience, according to Freud, is idealized because it is free from all dualisms...Psychoanalysis suggests the eschatological proposition that mankind will not put aside its sickness and its discontent until it is able to abolish every dualism.*

The ending of this statement is loaded with potential. Humanity *"will not put aside its sickness and its discontent until it is able to abolish every dualism."* This proposition means we must reconcile and heal all divisions—works of Diabalos, the divider—between religions, between science and religion, between Nature and us, and between one another. We are more than one nation under God. We are *all* a unity in the Godhead. This thesis transcends the notion of an individual nation. It reaches into the incomprehensible depths of intergalactic space and beyond.

In the INTRODUCTION to this book, I put forth my purpose in writing it: "*This book's purpose, then, is to bring peace through the integration of seemingly opposing forces.*" If you, dear reader, now see or are reinforced in your own conviction of the urgency of this mission, please join me in working for this deeper understanding of Peace. Not only is such peace necessary for humanity to "put aside its sickness and it discontent," to repeat Brown; it is also necessary for the survival of humanity and life as we know it on our planet. "The Peace that passes all understanding" (Philippians 4:7) is crucial to our salvation!

Here is where the great power of the Mother is revealed and needed most urgently. The Mother-Child relationship demolishes dualism. Author Nancy Verrier (1994, p. 29) says this beautifully:

> *The nature of the relationship between Mother and Child is characterized, not by subject and object, but a kind of fluidity of being, of Mother/Child/World transcending time and space. The Mother provides a container for the child's ego, just as she had previously provided the container for his developing physical body.*

Western science is just now beginning to remember our knowledge of unity through research on the relationship of a woman to her child. We are also remembering it through research on the relationship of humanity to Nature. Reflecting upon the latter, physicist John Wheeler (1979) states:

...So the old word 'observer' simply has to be crossed off the books and we must put in the new word 'participator.' In this way we've come to realize the universe is a participatory universe.

It is this participatory relationship that scholar E. Neumann (1973), who studies infancy, refers to as the *Participation Mystique*. This Participation Mystique illuminates the mystical, intuitive, and largely "unconscious" participation of a mother in the life of her infant and an infant in the life of her mother.

Considering current infant research, it appears the biological mother is specially prepared through bonding with her child, both in utero and upon birth, to meet the needs of the infant. These needs express themselves through intuition and other phenomena unobservable to anyone else (Verrier, 1994, p. 20). Researchers find that more than the palpable umbilical cord and breast milk bind child to mother and mother to child. Consider, for instance, how the shortened sleep periods of the mother, caused by the discomfort of her hugely enlarged belly and pressure on the bladder, bring the mother into correspondence with the neonatal infant's short sleep cycle. Think of how the mother's milk lets down when her infant is hungry, even when she is away from him. Think of how the properly bonded mother is able to interpret and respond to her infant's cries when they just sound like squalling to all other ears. Think of how the infant recognizes his mother's face, touch, and smell, differentiating her from all others. (Would that our society treasured and nurtured these bonds!)

This idea of ineffable mother-child bonding reflects the belief that the Universe is responsive to even our most subtle thoughts and feelings. Again, in science experiments, photons behave in accordance to the expectations of the experimenter. The scientist and the experiment are in a participatory relationship. Every relationship is a participatory transaction. A concept of God-the-Mother, together with a renewed appreciation and respect for human motherhood, is central to healing the alienation that causes fear, war, scarcity thinking, and the dualistic paradigm that plague and threaten to annihilate us.

Infant researchers Mahler and Neumann (1975) describe the relationship between Mother and Child as a *Dual Unity*. This mystical idea signifies that the mother acts as the child's Self in his infancy. She simultaneously *contains* the child's Self and *is* his Self. Why else would Nature be a Mother if she did not contain our Self? This is why Nature means essence. To highlight this Mother and Child relationship with Nature, let us return with fresh ears to the previously quoted words of the Hindu *Upanishads* (Campbell, 1974, p. 54):

> *It is below, it is above, it is to the west, it is to the east, it is to the south, it is to the north; it is, in fact, this entire world...And truly, the one who sees this, thinks this and understands this, takes pleasure in the Self, is joined to the Self, knows bliss in the Self; such a one is autonomous. He has unlimited freedom in all worlds.*

Knowing the concept these words convey definitely has ecological implications. How we treat the world is how we treat ourselves, because there are no distinctions between the world and ourselves. There is no universe out there with us in here. We are Nature. We can never be otherwise because Nature is our essence, our Self.

The entire world contains and unfolds as the Self. It is a mirror image of the biological mother who contains and is the self of her infant. There is a direct correlation between how we relate to our mother in infancy and how we relate to Nature as an adult. One of the ways you and I can most effectively work for peace is to honor, support, and give more than lip service to the high calling of motherhood. Every mother is a Priestess of Peace. If we give each mother the security, time, and respect she so richly deserves, our illusion/delusion of a distinction between subject and object will dissolve into the reality of diversity within unity. Warfare--whether interpersonal, intercultural, or international--will be seen as the unbearable travesty it truly is. Misogyny, with its attendant abuse and rape, will simply disappear. Every well-supported and cherished mother is her own holographic department of peace.

Within the past 20 years, there has been a trend towards the integration of Eastern philosophy into the West. Many see the East as providing an alternative to the stifling philosophies inherent in the linear, patriarchal, and reductionist values of Hellenistic European philosophy, science and religion. Even science began relating herself to Eastern philosophy, as illustrated through Capra's *The Tao of Physics* (1975).

However, when the West's symbols are stripped down to their core of original meanings, there are no essential distinctions between East and West. Truth is Truth no matter where we go. The West's Holy Spirit, originally known as the feminine Ruach and identified with Sophia, *is* the Oriental Shakti, meaning life, energy, wisdom and consciousness. These are not two ideas. The East and West are but two creative and unique manifestations of the same Spirit. They are different colors of the same rainbow emanating from the light of the Mother. There is no single religion that is correct. In their ground, every religion contains and unfolds as all other religions. Everything that exists, including the world's religions, are diverse manifestations or expressions, of the one Divine Reality in whom there is no other. In the Mother's depths, unity and diversity are not two. The answer to whether or not the universe is one or many is an astounding "Yes!" This is true of all dualisms, for we live in a "both/and" world more so than the "either /or" world depicted by our language.

Sophia's call in Proverbs 8:14 with which I introduced this chapter, is not to Jews, Christians, or Muslims. Her call is to all humanity. In her all is a seamless whole. She simultaneously sees through all events, peoples, and things. We serve simultaneously as her eyes, the manifestation that she sees, and the hologram of all that she is within her heart-of-hearts. Everything appears to her in its pure state: transparent and naked. She hears even the subtlest of thoughts for she is the origin and receiver of all things. Upon our ego's death into her, all forms–including our form–will reveal themselves as her forms. The entire universe will reveal itself as being contained in an infinite ocean of intelligence without boundaries. All will be as crystal clear as an unpolluted mountain stream. The reason we have such a problem with environmental pollution is that our minds are polluted! The one mirrors the other. Upon purifying our minds of greed and the need to dominate and control Nature, she will heal herself and us. These will not be two movements.

Ultimately, our Fate is to become what we already are, have always been, and always will be. To see into the belly of the Goddess who will devour us at the end of time, which is now, is to see into our Soul. We only need to turn our eyes inward. Ramakrishna (Hixon, 1992, p. 210) illustrates this idea below:

O' longing mind,
dwell within the Depths

of your own pure Nature.
Do not seek your home elsewhere.
Do not confine your innate Infinity
within the mansions of finitude.
Your naked Awareness alone, O' mind,
is the inexhaustible abundance
for which you long so desperately.

Become these words and you become Sophia. Let these words sing to you as you work, play, parent, sleep, eat and make love. Let them sing in everything you do. Become the Virgin. Become the Mother of God by birthing Love. Know her and him as your power, your bliss, your truth, and your enlightenment. Lose your pride and place your lips to her breasts. Take Love's phallus inside you. Truth will flow into your tummy like water. You will receive the "living water" that Christ promises.

YOU ARE ANOINTED BY GOD

Do not take my word for this. What do I know? Experience it firsthand. It might take some time and practice, but Sophia will eventually reveal herself when she has ripened you. The expert vineyard Queen only chooses grapes ripe enough for the enjoyment of her taste buds. To make yourself delicious and intoxicating for her enjoyment, lose yourself through deep meditation upon the infinite depths of your Soul. When you taste that purity, you will dissolve. Sweetness will dissolve into Sweetness with no remainder. Only the sweet bliss of Sophia's Womb of Pure Awareness will remain.

So, what is holding you back? Click your heels together three times, dive into the depths of your Soul, send your Wizard ego sailing off in his hot-air balloon, and awaken in Kansas as the Sleeping Beauty. When you awaken, you will know "Oz" was a dream; the wicked witch of the West (death) has melted; and the loving embrace of Auntie Em (Fate, Sophia) and Uncle Henry (the Ruler of the House) were with you the whole time. Like Bastian in *The Neverending Story,* you hold the whole ball of wax in your hands. Without your compassionate participation human-kind will perish from the Earth and with it the great gift of imagination.

Now-Here, with all its incumbent needs and challenges, is crucial to Eternity-Infinity. Give your whole heart, life, and labor to this moment in this place. ***You*** are an inherent, crucial microcosm of the All. The magnificent biblical claim, "God is Love," necessitates your being here-now for him to love and to love him and his creation reciprocally. Love is transitive in nature. Love is a verb as well as a noun; therefore, we must understand God as a verb as well as a noun. You MUST receive and give Love or all dissolves back into nothingness. God trusted you that much, with his own essence; his Holy Spirit, his Sophia, dwells in you. Do not let him down. That which you believe, accomplish, and manifest in this place and moment matters.

In closing, I pray Sophia (however you name the feminine divine) will shine her Light of Truth into the depths of your Soul. I also hope She does so in the eternal Present. I rededicate this book to Sophia and to all receptive readers. May it help you to BE the saving grace you were born to be! Amen.

Bibliography

Allen, Paula Gunn, *Grandmothers of the Light: A Medicine Woman's Sourcebook*, (Boston, MA: Beacon Press, 1991).

Apuleius, Lucius, *The Golden Ass*, (Tr.) Robert Graves, (New York, NY: The Noonday Press, 1992).

Arntz, William, Betsy Chasse, and Mark Vicente, *What the Bleep Do We Know!?*, (Lord of the Wind Films, LLC, 2004).

Austen, Hallie Inglehart, *The Heart of the Goddess*, (Oakland, CA: Wingbow Press, 1990).

Bateon, Gregory, *Steps to an Ecology of Mind*, (Ballantine Books, 2000).

Baring, Anne and Cashford, Jules, *Myth of the Goddess: Evolution of an Image*, (New York, NY: Pnguin Books, 1991).

Barnstone, Willis and Meyer, Marvin, *The Gnostic Bible: Gnostic Texts of Mystic Wisdom from the Ancient and Medieval Worlds*, (Boston, MA: Shambhala Publications, 2003).

Blair, Nancy, *Amulets of the Goddess*, (Oakland, CA: Wingbow Press, 1993).

Bohm, David, *Wholeness and the Implicate Order*, (New York, NY: Routledge Classics, 2002).

Bohm, David, *Thought as a System*, (New York, NY: Routledge Classics, 1994).

Briggs, John P. and Peat, F. David, *The Looking Glass Universe: The Emerging Science of Wholeness*, (New York, NY: Simon & Schuster, Inc., 1984).

Brown, Norman O., *Life Against Death: The Psychoanalytical Meaning of History,* (Middletown: Wesleyan Press, 1959).

Campbell, Joseph, *The Mythic Image,* (Princeton, NJ: Princeton University Press, 1974),

Campbell, Joseph, *The Hero With a Thousand Faces,* (Princeton, NJ: Princeton University Press, 1990).

Capra, Fritjof, *Uncommon Wisdom: Conversations with Remarkable People,* (New York, NY: Bantam Books, 1981).

Capra, Fritjof, *The Tao of Physics,* (Boston, MA: Shambhala, 1999).

Chopra, Deepak, *Ageless Body; Timeless Mind,* (New York, NY: Harmony Books, 1993).

Danielou, Alain, *Introduction to the Study of Musical Scales,* (London: India Society, 1943),

Danielou, Alain, *The Myths and Gods of India,* (Rochester, VT: Inner Traditions International, Ltd., 1991).

Doniger, Wendy (Tr), *The Rig Veda,* (New York, NY: Penguin Books, 1981).

Eisler, Riane, *The Chalice and the Blade: Our History, Our Future,* (New York, NY: HarperCollins Publishers, 1988).

Eisler, Riane, *Sacred Pleasure: The Myth and the Politics of the Body: New Paths to Power and Love,* (New York, NY: HarperCollins Publishers, 1996).

Ende, Michael, *The Neverending Story,* (New York, NY: Penguin Books USA, Inc, 1984).

Fox, Matthew, *Passion for Creation: Meister Eckhart's Creation Spirituality,* (New York, NY: Doubleday Dell Publishing Group, Inc, 1995).

Fox, Matthew, *The Coming of the Cosmic Christ,* (San Francisco, CA: HarperSanFrancisco, 1998).

Fox, Matthew, *Whee! Whee! Whee! All the Way Home: A Guide to Sensual, Prophetic Spirituality,* (Santa Fe, NM: Bear and Company, 1981).

Fromm, Eric, *Escape from Freedom,* (New York, NY: Henry Holt & Co., 1994).

Gimbutas, Marija, *The Goddesses and Gods of Old Europe,* (Berkley, CA: University of California Press, 1982).

Ginsburg, Yitzchak, *The Inner Dimension: Authentic Jewish Mysticism, Kabbalah and Chassidut,* (http://inner.org, 2005).

Goethe, Johann Wolfgang Von, *Faust: Part Two,* (Ed.) Phillip Wayne, (London, England: Penguin Classics, 1959),

Goethe, Johann, *Theory of Colours, paragraph #50* (1810).

Graves, Robert, *The White Goddess,* (New York, NY: The Noonday Press, 1948).

Grogan, John, *Marley and Me,* (New York, NY: HarperCollins Publisher, 2005).

Hall, Burl B., "The Fear of Ego Dissolution and the Suppression of Feminine Power," (Unpublished Manuscript presented at University of Texas, Arlington, 2000).

Hall, Meredith, "Rape of Gaia," (Unpublished Manuscript, 2006).

Hixon, Lex, *The Great Swan: Meetings with Ramakrishna,* (Boston, MA: Shambhala Publications, Inc., 1992).

Hixon, Lex, *Mother of the Universe: Visions of the Goddess and Tantric Hymns of Enlightenment,* (Wheaton, Ill: Quest Books, 1994).

Iyer, Raghaven, *The Jewel in the Lotus,* (London: The Pythagorean Sangha & Concord Press, 1988),

Jagger, Mick and Richards Keith, "Ruby Tuesday" appearing on *Through the Past Darkly* (ABKCO, 1969).

Jung, Carl, *The Portable Jung,* Edited by Campbell, Joseph (New York, NY: Penguin Books, 1976).

Katzenback, Maria, "The Ecopsychology of Oedipus," *Gatherings: Online Journal of the International Community of Ecopsychology,* (November, 2005).

Leet, Leonora, *The Secret Doctrine of the Kabbalah: Recovering the Key to Hebraic Sacred Science,* (Rochester, VT: Inner Traditions International, 1999).

Levy, Paul, *The Artist as Healer of the World* (www.awakenin-thedream.com/artis/artisthealer.html 2007).

Lovelock, James, *A Biography of Our Living Earth,* (New York, NY: W.W. Norton & Company, Inc, 1995).

Lysebeth Andre rican, *Tantra: The Cult of the Feminine,* (York Beach, ME: Samuel Weiser, Inc., 1995).

Mahler, M., Pine, F., & Bergman, A., *The Psychological Birth of the Human Infant,* (New York, NY: Basic Books, 1975).

Matthews, Caitlin, *Sophia: Goddess of Wisdom,* (London: The Aquarian Press, 1991).

Neuman, Eric, *The Great Mother,* (Princeton, NJ: Princeton University Press, 1983).

Neuman, Eric, *The Child,* (New York, NY: G.P. Putman, 1973).

Osho, *Tao: Its History and Teachings,* (East Sussex, UK: Ixos Press, 2005).

Peat, F. David, *Synchronicity: The Bridge Between Matter and Mind,* (New York, NY: Bantam Books, 1987).

Roszak, Theodore, *Voice of the Planet: An Exploration of Ecopsychology,* (York Beach, ME: Phanes Press, 2001).

Rumi, *The Illuminated Rumi,* (Tr.) Bankes, Coleman, (New York, NY: Broadway Books, 1997).

Ryan, Roma lyricist for Enja, "Pilgrim" appearing on *A Day Without Rain,* (Reprise / WEA, 2000).

Sagan, Carl, *Cosmos,* (New York, NY: Random House, 1980).

Schipflinger, Thomas, *Sophia-Maria: A Holistic Vision of Creation,* (York Beach, ME: Samuel Weiser, Inc., 1998).

Seamon David & Arthur Zajonc, editors, *Goethe's Way of Science: A Phenomenology of Nature,* (Albany, NY: State University of New York Press, 1998).

Siegel, Bernie, *Love, Medicine and Miracles: Lessons Learned About Self-Healing from a Surgeon's Experience with Exceptional Patients,* (New York, NY: Harper Collins Publishers, Inc., 1989).

Sheldrake, Rupert, *A New Science of Life,* (London: Blond and Briggs, 1981).

Spencer-Brown, G., *Laws of Form,* (New York, NY: Julian Press, 1972).

Solow, Andrew, R., "Red Tides and Dead Zones" http://www.whoi.edu/oceanus/viewArticle.do?id=2487

Steensma, Brian, http://www.gaianxaos.com/bio.htm.

Steiner, Rudolph, *The Etherisation of the Blood,* (London: Rudolf Steiner Press, 1911).

Talbot, Michael, *The Holographic Universe,* (New York, NY: HarperPerennial, 1991).

The Three Initiates, *The Kybalion: Hermetic Philosophy,* (Chicago, Ill: The Yogi Publication Society Masonic Temple, 1912).

Underhill, Evelyn, *Mysticism: The Preeminent Study in the Nature and Development of Spiritual Consciousness,* (New York, NY: Doubleday Dell Publishing Group, Inc., 1990).

Verrier, Nancy, *The Primal Wound: Understanding the Adopted Child,* (Baltimore, MD: Gateway Pres, Inc., 1994).

Walkers, Barbara, *The Woman's Encyclopedia of Myths and Secrets,* (New York, NY: HarperCollins Publishers, Inc., 1983).

Watts, Alan, *The Tao of Philosophy,* (Ed.: Mark Watts, London: Tuttle Publishing, 1995).

West, John Anthony, *The Serpent in the Sky: The High Wisdom of Ancient Egypt,* (Wheaton, Ill: Quest Books, 1993).

Wheeler, J.A. in Buckley, Paul and Peat, F. David, *A Question of Physics,* (London: Routledge and Kegan Paul, 1979).

White, E. B., *Charlotte's Web,* (New York: HarperCollins, 1952).

Wilber, Ken, *Spectrum of Consciousness,* (Wheaton, Ill: Theological Publishing House, 1993).

Wilber, Ken, *Official Website,* (www.kenwilber.com, 2004).

Wolf, Fred Allen, *Mind into Matter: A New Alchemy of Science and Spirit,* (Portsmouth, NH: Moment Point Press, 2001).